All about the
Racing Greyhound

All about the Racing Greyhound

BARBARA TOMPKINS
PAM HEASMAN

PELHAM BOOKS
London

Published by the Penguin Group
27 Wrights Lane, London W8 5TZ, England
Viking Penguin Inc., 40 West 23rd Street, New York, New York 10010, USA
Penguin Books Australia Ltd, Ringwood, Victoria, Australia
Penguin Books Canada Ltd, 2801 John Street, Markham, Ontario, Canada L3R 1B4
Penguin Books (NZ) Ltd, 182–190 Wairau Road, Auckland 10, New Zealand

Penguin Books Ltd, Registered Offices: Harmondsworth, Middlesex, England

First published 1988

British Library Cataloguing in Publication Data

Tompkins, Barbara
　All about the racing greyhound.
　1. Greyhounds. Breeding & training
　I. Title　　II. Heasman, Pam
　636.7′53

　ISBN 0–7207–1767–1

Credits

The authors and publishers are grateful to the following for permission to reproduce copyright
photographs:
J. A. Ballard pages 147, 151, 153: Dodds page 56; *Evening Standard* pages 35, 38; Greyhound
Racing Association pages 21, 24; Brendan Hackett page 146; Neil Martin page 102; Stephen Nash
pages 4, 7, 8, 14, 15, 16, 17, 28, 30, 31, 33, 37, 41, 51, 52, 60, 63, 78, 83, 94, 95, 96, 97, 103, 106,
108, 119, 150, 158, 160, 163; NB Photos page 148; Turvey and Turvey page 164. Figures 3, 4, 5
and 6 are reproduced from INTRODUCTION TO THE FUNCTIONAL ANATOMY OF
THE LIMBS OF THE DOMESTIC ANIMAL published by John Wright and Sons Ltd.
Figures 1 and 7 are drawn by Pan Tek.

Made and printed in Great Britain by
Butler & Tanner Ltd, Frome and London

Contents

Acknowledgements

The authors are most grateful to the help given to them in the sections on injuries and worms by Carol Nicholson MRCVS.

1   The Pros and Cons of Owning a Racing Greyhound

What many people do not realise when they decide to own and train a racing Greyhound is that it's not like owning a piece of furniture – you can't put it carefully in the corner, dust it every so often and stand back and admire it. In the back yard or the back garden in a kennel is 'another member of the family'. This member expects to be fed twice a day with the correct diet to keep him fit and healthy, and needs proper exercise, grooming, galloping and all the other little things that go towards getting fit to win a race.

Now all these requirements not only cost a certain amount of money but also involve a large amount of what is called 'dedication'. Every day you will have to do the same things, like getting up in the morning an hour before your usual time, going out in the pouring rain, perhaps, to take your dog for a walk, cleaning out the kennel and serving up the breakfast that he is waiting for. All this before you have your own, and whether or not you have a 'hang over'.

Unless you can truthfully say, 'Yes, this is what I am interested in,' and you realise that you are not entering a 'get-rich-quick' sport, then you are wasting your time and money joining the Greyhound racing fraternity.

Having made the decision that you really want a racing Greyhound, then the choice is yours as to whether to have a puppy and rear him yourself, or buy a dog that is schooled and ready to go to the track for his grading trials.

There is nothing more exciting once you have made your decision than to go to the kennel in the morning and be greeted by leaping pups with happy faces and bright eyes, delighted to see you and raring to go.

The economics of the game are quite important in making your choice. If you buy a puppy at about ten weeks old, when his earmarking has been done and he has received the necessary inoculations, a well-bred, well-started animal could cost you anything from £350 to, say, £500. On top of this initial outlay you will have to keep and feed your pup until he is twelve months of age before he can start his schooling. Then, if everything goes according to plan, it will be another two to three months before he is really old enough to race.

Let's now look at the costs involved in this operation. First, there is the purchase price, plus something in the region of a minimum of £12 per week to feed and generally service the pup. The cost of schooling can be cut if you are able to do some of this yourself, provided there is a good, safe schooling track within reasonable reach. If the pup takes to the track well and you have no problems then you might assume you are 'in clover', as they say. However, whichever way you look at the costs there will not be much change from £1000, if any! But on the credit side, you will have paid out this money in fairly easy stages.

I feel that the schooling angle should be given quite a lot of thought before the time comes for it to begin. A puppy reared on his own is inclined to get too soft and, on balance, it is a good idea to send him away for his schooling. This way he will get used to proper kennelling and to being handled by people other than his owners. However, this will be discussed in more detail in a later chapter.

To buy a dog that is already racing is perhaps more difficult and there are two very important points that need looking into carefully.

The first is to try to make sure that the dog you are buying is sound. To do this it is quite useful to obtain some expert help. Some injuries, such as damaged toes, tendons, fractured hocks or swellings where there should be none, will be obvious but old injuries, perhaps in the muscles, may not be so easy to spot. If you are buying at a sale watch the sales trials carefully; some muscle injuries will show themselves in the way a dog takes the first bend, by whether he runs off or checks. 'Running off' means that instead of going round the bend, more or less following the line that he started on and following the line of the bend, he will appear to be going to run straight on. 'Checking' means that you see the dog hesitate for a second, almost as if he is going to stop dead. Another good pointer is the way his tail behaves. If you see a dog's tail go up at the bend you can almost be sure that he is lame somewhere. There is always a veterinary surgeon at the sales and it would be a good idea to ask him to go over any dog that you are interested in after it has had its trial.

The second point to watch for is the 'dodge'. There are many ways of being not quite honest, apart from out and out fighting. Some dogs will catch the leading dog and stay with it. If they seem to catch the leader easily but take a very long time to go past it, or never do, they would be the kind to avoid.

Also, watch for the dog who takes the lead in a trial in great style, but, when he gets to about a length in front, eases off and waits for those behind to catch up. Once he has company again he will go on. The trouble with dogs such as these is that they are so busy wondering where the others are they frequently get beaten on the line. These are examples of the easily spotted 'dodges'. Others are not so apparent and you have to see a dog run a few times before you can be sure that he is just trundling along with the pack and not doing his best for one reason or another.

When buying a dog that is already racing, it is usually better to buy a young one of, say, sixteen to twenty-two months old. They are the sort who will improve with experience and age, and, with any luck and no injuries, will give you between eighteen months' and two years' racing. I must confess here that I have a great feeling for the older dog. Sometimes you come across a dog of perhaps two and a half or three years old who is quite sound but has obviously had a bad home. His skin will be in bad condition and he will be far too light; he will also have that tired look about him. Such dogs can quite often be bought for next to nothing. Give him some decent food, a good bed and some genuine kindness, and you will be surprised how he will come back and run for you. However, when opting for a dog like this, try to find out about his background and whether he was ever a decent dog with a bit of pace and not always plagued with injury, no matter how trivial.

Look at the economics of this option. Young dogs, and old ones for that matter, can quite often be bought inexpensively at the sales, for about £100 to £300, and can give you endless pleasure and win races. When you are watching the trials look for a dog who seems to be able to accelerate when coming off the second bend or up the back straight. It does not matter if he loses the trial as long as he shows some track craft or speed somewhere during his run.

When buying an older dog who is already running on the track, either from the sales or from a trainer, it is a good idea not to buy a very shy dog. This applies more particularly to a bitch. Nerves like that are hereditary and should you wish to breed from your bitch at a later date you will surely get some very shy puppies. However, it is quite natural for a dog to back away fractionally from two or three strangers crowding round him. If you step into the dog's 'shoes', as it were, and imagine yourself in his situation, you too would feel a bit apprehensive and wonder what was going to happen. The ones to avoid are those who go quite scatty in their efforts to get away from strangers, perhaps even trying to bite at times.

To go back to the choices. Perhaps you feel that you would really rather buy a pup, watch it grow and dream about the day he turns out to be a Derby winner (which we all do). Then you should now think about choosing the pup that you are going to rear.

First, select the litter that you wish to go and look at, by studying the breeding and making enquiries regarding the performance of the parents. Then contact the breeder to make arrangements to inspect the pups.

In my opinion it is not a good idea to visit them when they are too young. However, with the present rules regarding earmarking, the litter generally stay together until they are between ten and twelve weeks old. I feel that seven to eight weeks is a good time to have a look. The pups will be well weaned and running about outside by that time. You will be able to pick out the gay and happy pup who is not a bully but has a kind eye and is pleased to see visitors. Avoid the very shy type, who run and hide whenever anybody strange arrives.

To look at pups properly you must give yourself time to watch them play for quite a while. This gives some insight into the character of the individual, and allows you to see how they move. Pups need to move well, whatever their age. It can be seen whether they have a good long stride, whether they are badly cow-hocked or indeed whether their legs go in all directions instead of fairly straight. The illustrations show some of the faults to avoid. Of course, perfect movement at this age is

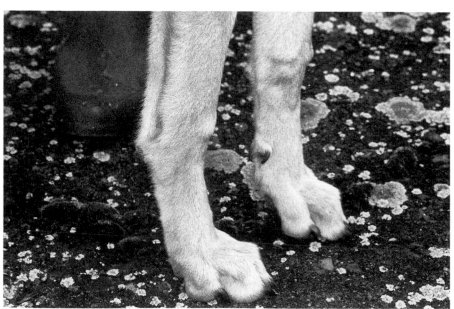

A puppy's legs showing good strong bone.

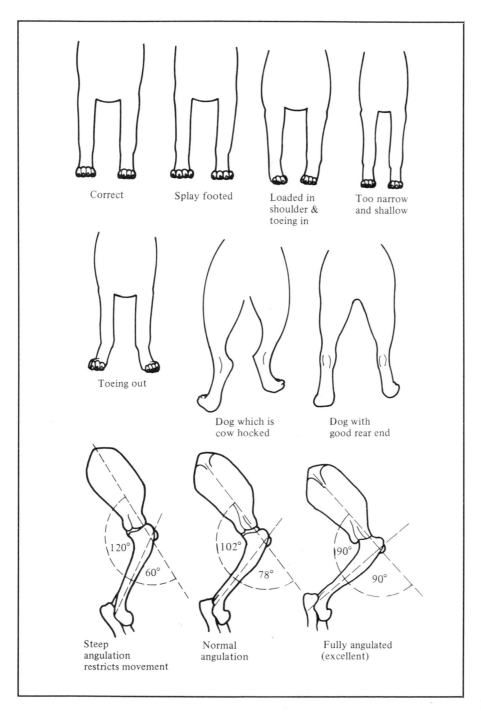

Fig. 1 Common Faults.

very unusual as pups tend to 'bumble' about, but by watching them carefully you can get a fair idea of the finished product. Look out for good bone and feet. Puppies need to have nice knobbly knees because the growth comes from the knobbles! The legs should be straight (any 'bowing' in the limbs at that age indicates the start of rickets) and the feet tight, by which I mean well shaped, like a cat's, and not too long in the toes, since very long toes break easily.

It is very important to look at the pups' mouths since some Greyhounds seem to suffer from 'pig mouth', which in severe cases restricts their feeding. Small irregularities don't matter too much but a correct bite is preferable. (See illustration.) The pups should have a decent covering of flesh and should have been wormed at least twice for roundworms by that time.

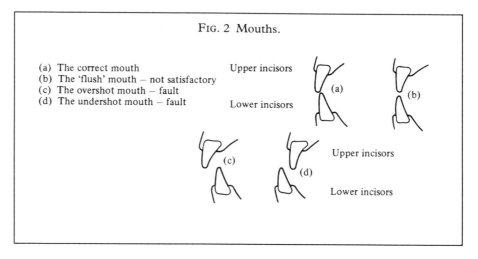

FIG. 2 Mouths.

(a) The correct mouth
(b) The 'flush' mouth – not satisfactory
(c) The overshot mouth – fault
(d) The undershot mouth – fault

Upper incisors

Lower incisors

Upper incisors

Lower incisors

Some people say that colour is important, but the old adage that 'no good horse is a bad colour' applies to Greyhounds too. Many people hate blues but, personally, I love them. I have had two or three terrific blues and I suppose one gets slightly biased! Honestly, though, colour is not that important.

The pups will have to stay together until the earmarking is done. However, you can pick the one you fancy and make the necessary arrangements with the breeder to collect it in due course. If, when you return to pick up your puppy, you discover that the earmarking has obviously caused excessive stress problems, then perhaps it would be better to change or leave the pup with the breeder for an extra week so that it can stay with its friends a bit longer.

Some people say that it is not a good idea to rear one pup on its own.

Pam and I don't entirely agree on this point. It is generally accepted that two pups do better than one because in a pair they develop competitiveness, which is a very important trait in the Greyhound. But I have an open mind about this; I think it depends on how much contact with people the pup gets. If you have a pet dog in the house it's not a bad idea to let the young Greyhound 'pal up' with it from an early age. Pups need company, and it must be provided in some form or other. I shall go into this in more detail in Chapter 2.

This well-boned, well-fleshed litter of puppies are still together at 10 weeks.

2 Rearing Puppies

Before you bring your pup home arrangements should be made for its housing and the provision of an exercise paddock. If you are keeping it at home you might choose to buy a purpose-built kennel from one of the firms who advertise in the dog papers. These can be obtained with benches and windows and all the necessary requirements. They can be erected at the bottom of the garden with a fenced paddock surround so that the pup can run in and out of the house at will. The larger the paddock the better because even at an early age the pup needs to have a good deal of freedom. If that part of the garden happens to have one or two trees, so much the better. Puppies love to play round the trees and it teaches them to use themselves.

If, on the other hand, you happen to have a brick-built shed or barn that can easily be adapted, that can be very useful. Make sure, however, that a wooden bench is fitted in the sleeping quarter, about 12 ins (30 cm) off the floor, and it is a good idea to line the walls of the bench area with some good plywood. If you put the wood on a frame have it about 2 ft 6 ins (75 cm) high, when the weather gets very cold you can rest a piece of plywood on top so it forms a kind of box. This is very cosy for the pup and will keep him lovely and warm. If you have two pups make sure that the bed area is big enough. For two you would need an area 5 ft (150 cm) long by 3 ft 6 ins (105 cm) deep.

Concrete floors can be very cold in winter, so always put a good covering of nice clean sawdust on the floor in the pen area in front of the bed. One well-known lady breeder who rears a lot of pups says that a good covering of sawdust on the floor is as good as an extra meal. She is right; it keeps the cold from striking up and makes everywhere feel altogether warmer. Here again the paddock area needs to be attached to the building in some way.

Bedding can be provided using either good clean straw or shredded paper, both of which are readily available. Make sure that the straw is dry and clean and as long as possible; the paper, on the other hand,

(OPPOSITE)
An alert puppy at 10 weeks.

should not be long as it can wrap itself round a dog's feet and cause a problem – it can get very tight and stop the circulation in the foot.

I use shredded computer paper, which tends to be long but can be easily pulled out and torn off at about 12–18 in. (30–45 cm) lengths.

The bedding should be changed at least once a week, otherwise it gets smelly and tends to harbour 'visitors', such as fleas and lice.

When rearing a pup at home there is usually an area of grass where you can go for your exercise. To start with, let the pup run about at will. He won't overdo it as pups seem to know when they have had enough. Young Greyhounds do not want overstraining and forcing to gallop. Running round in circles and weaving about, which they do quite naturally, teaches them to use themselves, and this is far more beneficial in the early days than running them up a straight gallop from one person to another. Lead training at an early age is a must, they get very upset if it is introduced when they are older.

Many people advocate a lot of road work for Greyhounds. They seem to forget that a pup is not yet mature enough to take on such work. Until the pup is about seven months old road work ought to be restricted to about a mile per day, and that is plenty. Take your pup over the fields on the lead by all means, but then let him do his own thing, running round. If you happen to be rearing two pups together it is not a good thing to let them run about as a pair. Obviously they are going to play together in their paddock, but when you have them out and you want them to really have a gallop it's better to let them off separately. If you don't, they get into the habit of playing and chasing each other and when you come to school them this can lead to 'leaning on' which, although the pups are only playing, can be construed as fighting. Anyway, it's a bad habit and should be avoided if possible.

Feeding puppies is quite a controversial subject and one that I must confess I am rather old-fashioned about whereas Pam is not. However, we agree that everyone should do things the way they feel is best for them, so here we can only give the alternatives. To start with, pups of about twelve weeks old will still require three meals a day. The reason for this is that if they are given very large meals they get a distended stomach, so the meals have to be split up. We shall assume that their breakfast will be served somewhere between 7 and 8 am and start from there.

Diet sheets for various ages will be found in Appendix A as well as details of supplements. These latter are very important and should be chosen carefully, particularly the ones for growing pups. As far as the diets are concerned, there is no hard and fast rule about which one is best. The examples we have given are all suitable and it is the one which fits in with your routine that you should use. Do remember, though, that the pups are growing all the time and you will need to increase the quantities of meat or expanded food as they grow.

However, don't be like the farmer's boy who was feeding the cattle. The farmer found that his beasts were not clearing up their food and guessed the reason. So he arranged with his wife to play a little trick to bring the lesson home to his boy. At breakfast one morning she piled his plate up with porridge, and as soon as he finished that she put some more in. This went on until eventually the boy cried, 'Halt.' He could eat no more and felt positively ill. So the farmer said to him, 'Now that is how the beasts feel when you constantly overfeed them.' The point is: when pups start to leave food give them a rest. I always give one meal of bread and milk a week. This is done with the racing dogs as well as the pups. On that day they get no breakfast and just the one meal in the middle of the day. It serves to cleanse their systems, and when dogs are having a lot of raw meat it gets rid of excess bile.

There are quite a number of good expanded foods on the market which can be successfully fed to pups as their staple diet. Some of these foods are higher in protein than others. When using any of the 27–29% varieties for pups it is not necessary to feed any meat or vegetables because everything is in the mix and it is balanced. Do, however, feed according to the maker's instruction and make sure, if you are going to use the soaking method, that you soak for long enough and with adequate hot water or boiling soup so that some of the heat stays in the food during the soaking period. All the different makes of this type of food can be found in Appendix A.

These foods are very labour-saving insomuch as they cut out the preparation and cooking of meat and tripe. I used to call them 'lazy' foods but I have seen a number of pups reared this way and, to be quite honest, I could not fault them.

It must, however, be remembered that there is no substitute for milk for growing pups and it must always be fed *ad lib* until the pups are six months old. If you can obtain enough goats' milk then there is nothing to beat it. The most widely used milk substitute is Litter Lac, which is very good. The different types of milk and their nutritive breakdowns can be found in Appendix A.

If it is not possible to rear your own puppy, there are quite a few places in England and Wales which will take in pups to rear. Before you engage the services of such an establishment I would suggest that you visit a few of them and see exactly what they are like. Look at the pups who are already there; note whether they seem nervous or are in bad condition. Pay particular attention to whether the place looks clean and the paddocks are not obviously full of excreta, etc.

Have a look at the food they are feeding. You could even arrange to arrive at feeding time, which is rather sneaky I suppose, but you can then get an idea of whether the pups are getting enough to eat, whether the dishes are clean and whether the food looks fresh and nice. The average price for rearing is about £12 per week, and I imagine it goes up as the pup grows. Beware of anything too cheap; it stands to reason that it would be impossible to feed a pup properly on a low budget. Very often someone will recommend a good place, but, even so, go and see for yourself.

There is just one other point about rearing pups at home, which applies particularly if you happen to live in a town or village. If you take your pups to exercise on playing fields or some other public open space do try to get them to empty themselves in the paddock at home before you go out. Currently there is a great deal of bad press for dogs, in local and national papers, regarding 'dog mess' where other people walk. There is nothing worse than this, and I think every dog owner should take a responsible attitude to the problem. Also make sure that there are no other dogs about, particularly small ones, when you let your pups loose for a gallop – they may be only playing but they can give other owners terrible frights, which is not kind.

3 Schooling

When your pup has attained the great age of twelve months, he can, at last, commence his schooling. I hope that while you have been rearing your pup all those months you have taken the trouble to find out what the word 'schooling' means.

Before you go to the schooling track, the puppy should have been out and about in places where he will have encountered some live rabbits running freely. It's not too difficult to find a farmer who will let you walk on his land, provided that you are sensible and don't 'course' the sheep. A few runs after a rabbit or young hare will do the world of good and get the idea of chasing into the pup's head.

Schooling is an introduction to the track, and begins by taking the pup to a trial and letting it have a look to see what goes on. Travelling is an important part of the training as well. On the whole, Greyhounds are good travellers, but you do meet the exception to the rule.

For the first couple of times it is best to just hold the pup carefully on the lead and allow it to watch the hare go round. Quite often the manager of the track will, if asked, let you stand in the middle of the arena, so that the pup can see the track all round. If you do this, please make sure that the pup cannot slip his collar. There is nothing more dangerous and annoying to the hare driver than a loose dog rushing around the inside, trying to jump the fence onto the track, upsetting the trial that is being run. The danger is, of course, that the pup will get onto the track and get tangled up with the hare rope, from which exercise it will receive some terrible injuries. People do not understand that it is impossible to stop the hare dead, however hard the driver tries. The dilemma is always whether to stop the hare and risk the dogs in the trial hitting the hare arm and injuring themselves, or whether to carry on (while saying your prayers) and hope that the loose dog keeps out of the way.

You may find that the pup seems terribly keen, and the temptation is always there to 'let him have a go', but you should not do this. Wait,

(ABOVE AND OPPOSITE)
The correct way to
handslip a puppy.

take him home and go again the next week. Do the same thing the next
time. When you go on the third occasion it would be right to 'let him
have a go'. Take him onto the track between the sprint traps and the
first bend, and handslip him. When you handslip a dog, remove the
collar and lead, and, with your left arm round his neck and your right
arm under his tummy, hold him firmly while you wait for the hare to
come round (see illustration).

When the hare goes past and is about 15 yards (15 m) up, let your
pup go. Hopefully he will give chase. If he does, then run back to the
'trip' where the hare stops and be there with plenty of praise and a
'dummy' for him to jump on. Dummies can be very easily made from
a bit of fur fabric filled with soft stuffing and a couple of those rubber
toys that squeak sewn inside. Pups love that. It's the same sort of thing
as the reward system when training for obedience work; they look
forward to getting the 'dummy' at the end.

First time in the traps.   When the pup has become used to going round the track and is chasing well, then you can introduce the traps. We usually shut the front down and for the first time hold him in the trap with the back door open. When the hare comes round and the person operating the traps pulls the lever and opens them, we give the pup a push. Even if the pup is slow he soon gets the idea, and when you shut the back door the next time he usually improves in getting out. Some people advocate leaving the front of the trap up the first time, holding the dog in and

then letting him go when the hare comes round. That is very good for a dog that is not 'dead keen'. When you get a very keen dog, the minute he hears the hare he wants to be off and then you have a hell of a job trying to hang on to him. If he gets away it can cause a serious accident.

It is not wise to get your pup 'fighting fit' before you start schooling. The very fact that he is doing something quite new soon fines him down. So, have a good back, by which I mean plenty of flesh on the pup, before you start. It will come off fast enough and he will run himself fit.

There are some pups who show absolutely no interest at all in the track nor the hare when they first see it. These are some of the more difficult ones.

If this is the case it's quite a good idea, if you live in the country, to find a farmer who will let you walk his fields. Let the pup poke about in the hedge bottoms and it will quite likely put up a rabbit and have a chase. The main point is that you have to develop in the pup the will to 'chase'. It's a natural instinct in a Greyhound and should not be too hard to find. Sometimes the exercise has to be repeated a few times. Once you have managed to arouse his interest in hunting take the pup back to the track and go through all the early procedure again. Hopefully it will work and then you go on from there.

Some people attach a lure to a long string with the power provided by a bike wheel or a battery. They run the pups up a straight just to get them to chase. This works well usually, but don't do it too many times, otherwise when you come to try them on the track you may find that when they get to the bend and the hare goes round it they turn around because bends are not on their 'menu'! One of the dangers of too much 'straight work' is very simply that it can lead to some very bad injuries. The pup is so used to getting up speed on a straight gallop that when it gets to the bend it immediately becomes completely unbalanced. It can hit the outside rail because it is not able to get round the bend, or it can put an enormous strain on its muscles and bones which at twelve months are not really set properly anyway. We have seen broken hocks and very bad shoulders resulting from this practice. This can lead to a lot of problems, and very often the pup has to be handslipped behind another to give him the idea that he must follow round the bend.

When a pup has been reared on its own at home it tends to get 'caded', in other words too attached to its owners. If this is the case it quite often poses problems when it comes to schooling time. Should you feel that the pup might be too attached to you, one way to try to overcome this is to let the person on the traps do the first handslip. While that is in progress it is a good idea for you to get out of the way so the pup cannot see you. It does lessen the chance that it will run back to you. If, however, this does not work and the pup persists in running back then I recommend that you put it in kennels to receive professional schooling.

The large majority of dogs that are sent to schooling kennels go there because, for one reason or another, they will not chase. I would suggest that they are left in the kennels for at least four weeks. It is not possible to do much with difficult pups in under that time, and it quite often takes longer. To start with, they need a week or more to settle down before the trainer can think about taking them on the track to do any work. The main problem is that some of them refuse to eat for the first few days and, until you have got them feeding properly, it's pointless to go any further. Some develop a latent nervous streak and become difficult to catch, so they have to be contained in a small paddock until they get over it. I have known it take over a month to get a pup from the kennel to the track. This is unusual but it can happen. Owners tend to think that the trainer has left the dog to 'lie on the bed' and done nothing. This is not so, and you have to look at the other side of the coin.

What if the trainer were to loose the dog and it ran off and he couldn't catch it. What does he do? He can't take the risk of the dog running onto the road and being killed. What can he say to the owner? He has to tell the owner the truth, but the owner is not going to be very pleased – after all, the owner has reared the dog from puppyhood and has always been able to catch it. So the trainer gets labelled a 'bloody fool' and loses his reputation through no fault of his own.

Owners need to think about these points. If they are prepared to put the dog into a schooling establishment with someone who has been recommended or whom they know, it's best to leave the job to them. Don't keep going to see the dog. This merely upsets the animal and the trainer has then the hassle of an unsettled puppy to contend with all over again. Telephone in the evening, and you will always get a progress report that way.

Don't be discouraged if the puppy won't run the first few times. Some of them can be very difficult until the 'penny drops'. Mind you, there a few that never make it, and there are a few who turn out to be fighters, however careful you are with the rearing and subsequent schooling.

My personal view is that if you have a reluctant puppy that continually turns round and comes back, or indeed refuses to go at all, it is a mistake to allow this syndrome to continue for too long. Most schooling establishments have an old dog or bitch to take that kind round. Very often a pup will follow another dog round, and if this is done two or three times, it gets the idea that it is expected to arrive at the trip. It is better if it goes on its own, but if it won't, other measures have to be taken.

We once had to school a pup who absolutely refused to take any interest at all. The owner was very patient – he kept paying the bills, and we kept saying he was wasting his money. However, in the end, after about thirty trials running behind another dog, one day he suddenly flew past and won the trial. We had cracked it! That dog never looked back; he went away and won countless races for his very long-suffering owner. Mind you, the man deserved everything the dog did for him.

Another very important point about schooling is to decide which hare you should start the pup on. It's not a bad idea to have a plan in your mind about what the pup's future holds. If you are mostly going in for independent racing then the Inside Sumner Hare is the one that most independent tracks have. So start your pup on that one. If, on the other hand, you wish to race the pup under rules, either permit or on a fully licensed NGRC track, start the schooling on the outside hare. Quite a number of schooling tracks have an Outside Sumner Hare, so opt for one of those.

It is very important to teach the pup during the schooling period to chase all types of hare. The other important point is that most NGRC tracks have the McGee-type hare. The difference here is that the McGee runs on a track set in the ground and actually looks more like a hare. The Sumner-type hares are on an arm and move along off the ground. Puppies can get too used to one type of hare and then won't chase anything else properly. This can be witnessed in the number of Irish dogs who will not chase an Inside Sumner. They have no inside hares in Ireland so the dogs have never seen one. Also, the only outside Sumner in Ireland is at Dungannon, the remainder being the McGee type.

At about nine months old your pup needs to have its papers attended to. When you bought the pup the breeder should have given you a Green Form. On this form is stamped the earmark of the dog. This is done by the earmarking steward when he earmarks the pup. The form should be signed by the breeder and you should make sure that the earmark on the pup is the same one as on the form. These forms are more or less self-explanatory.

This green form is the naming form. You must name the pup before it is twelve months old, otherwise you run into 'fines' for being late. When you do the naming and send the form away to the Greyhound Stud Book, they will send back a white form with a marking diagram. The trainer at the schooling track will almost certainly be able to help you with the marking up of the pup. Don't forget to sign the form in

Reg Young with John
Silver, the 1970 Derby
winner.

all the relevant places otherwise it will be sent back. The Greyhound Stud Book will then send you a book with the white form attached inside.

If you are going to run your pup under rules, this book has to be presented to the racing manager and he will then mark the pup up again for the NGRC. Once all this is done the pup can then have its trials under rules.

The other type of registration paper that might accompany your pup when you buy him is the Irish Coursing Club naming form. Some breeders do not register their bitches with the Greyhound Stud Book and if the bitch originally came from Ireland the papers will be Irish. The procedure is more or less the same except that the forms have to be sent to Clonmel, and they send the marking forms to you. The only difference is that the marking of the puppy on the Irish form that you first receive must be done by an NGRC licensed official.

4 Training

A trainer is one who improves and prepares men, horses or dogs for athletic feats. Note the word 'improve'. This says it all. This is the difference between a trainer and a kennel keeper, and is the art of the game. As a trainer your job is not to rack your brains for a way to pull 'strokes' over the racing manager but to get your dog graded fairly and then to improve him to win the race that you are in.

There are too many people today who think that gambling is the beginning and end of dog racing. It is not. It may be so for some owners but it should not be for the trainer. That part of the game is not the trainer's concern. You, as the trainer, are there to get the best from your dog by feeding, exercise and discipline, which really means routine.

Perhaps we should start with routine. This is the most important part of running a racing kennel. Dependent on the weather, you must start attending your dogs in the morning at a certain time. In the summer it is a good thing to begin at about 6.30 am, and in the winter at 8 am. This seems a big difference, but in the cold and wet weather of the wintertime the dogs don't want to get up in the dark and go out in the cold before the streets are 'aired', as it were. In the summer even if it does rain it's not cold rain, it gets light early and the dogs like to be out walking the fields looking at anything that moves. Once you have established your time to start it has to be adhered to because the dogs get used to it. They seem to have inbuilt clocks and to them time is important. An easy timetable for the day is as follows:

6.30 am Put dogs in the paddock while you empty and clean the kennels. Shake up the beds, checking for wet or, if you have any dogs off colour, vomit. Once you have smelt vomit you will always notice it again – as soon as you go into the kennel that rather nasty sour smell is present. Dogs have a habit of being sick and covering it up with bedding, so unless the beds are properly shaken up it can be missed.

It is best to use good white sawdust for the floors in the kennels.

Some people like to wash out, saturating everywhere with water. In the winter this makes the kennels very cold and the floors never dry. The dogs' feet are always wet, which can lead to forms of foot rot, and also the beds are always damp where the dogs jump on and off them taking the water with them. In the summer the floors may dry eventually but the water makes the kennels humid and, again, the beds are always damp. Have a decent semi-hard brush that you can poke into the corners to remove all the wet sawdust. If this is done properly every day, there is really no smell at all.

It's not a bad thing, if you have a kennel empty for a day or two, to scrub the floor then. I use a solution of bleach, which is as good as anything for killing germs, but be sure that the surplus water is brushed out and that no dogs are put in until the floor is properly dry.

7.00 am   Walking.

8.00 am   Prepare and give breakfast to the dogs and to yourself.

9.00 am   Cookhouse chores and any other jobs that require doing around about the kennel. During this time the dogs will rest.

10.00 am–1.00 pm   Grooming, galloping and the 'sick and lame parade'. Any bandages that need changing or feet that need soaking and dressing can be attended to during this time. Sick dogs can be given their medication, etc.

1.00–2.00 pm   Lunch hour.

2.00 pm   Afternoon exercise.

3.30 pm   Prepare to feed.

4.00 pm   Feed the dogs and put them in the paddocks again to empty if they will. This does save a lot of mess in the kennels in the morning. If you have any really good dogs, it is a good thing in the summer to let them out again or take them for a little walk at about 8.30 pm. They will rest better perhaps and it serves to strengthen the bond between you and the dog if he has a bit of attention to himself. You do not want to make pampered pets of Greyhounds but it is a good thing to be friends with them. Just before the kennels are shut up for the night it does no harm to go round and speak to all the dogs individually, going into the kennel and giving them a bit of fuss. You notice then any that are unhappy for some reason or other. The sure sign of a contented Greyhound is when, after he has had his food, you see him lying on his back with all four feet in the air, completely relaxed.

(OPPOSITE)
Tilbrook Herald, winner of the British Breeders Stakes 1975.

The important thing with any animals is to know them well and observe them closely. Far too many people look at their dogs in a vague sort of way and don't notice the little things that very often make the difference between winning and losing races.

This timetable may not suit everybody, but it is an example of a routine that would work very well in a large Greyhound kennel. For those trainers who have to do a job as well as look after their dogs, this system would not work unless they were able to enlist the help of their long-suffering wives or husbands. Basically you must work your kennel to suit yourself, but however it is done the point about trying to stick to a timetable is very important.

Many a final has been lost through upsetting the routine of a dog. People seem to think that in the last week before a final they have to step up the training and anything else they can think of. One hears of trainers arriving at the track on a final night telling everyone what a lot of work they have done with the dog during the week. The result of this is that both the trainer and the dog look and feel like a wet week.

Your dog should be fit on semi-final night. The art of finals is to keep your dog on top for that last week, keep his weight exactly right, and just put the final polish on. Whatever happens try not to give way to nerves. Everyone has them and it tends to turn them into bad-tempered idiots. Also, this affects the dogs; they always seem to know when one is nervous and it unsettles them. Normally good owners (if you are training for other people) start behaving like a hen with a large brood of chicks; they tend to haunt you and the telephone rings constantly. It's either them or the press. One has to try and be polite to the press because at the present time Greyhound racing needs all the coverage it can get, and, of course, you can sympathise with the owners. I had one owner with a Derby finalist whose wife was a devout Catholic. She sent a bottle of Holy Water over with instructions that the dog should be sprinkled daily. I did what she said because the dog had two large tendons and a problem in a hind muscle and to win the Derby we would have had to have some Divine help! So the week was spent with a bottle of comfrey oil in one hand and Holy Water in the other. Needless to say we did not win, although the dog ran well enough considering all its handicaps.

Keep your head and your feet firmly on the ground, and if your dog is good enough and you have a bit of luck you will win.

We have touched on feeding in an earlier chapter, but that was mainly feeding puppies. A racing dog's diet is also a very controversial subject. Quite a few people still feed the old-fashioned way, but many now have gone on to expanded foods, details of which can be found in Appendix A.

Normally a racing dog's breakfast consists of cereal (e.g. Weetabix, or brown bread toasted), white of egg, glucose and milk. The amounts vary according to the dog's weight, and it is only through trial and error that one can get the amount right. Many trainers will not use eggs at all; they are fattening and I never use the whole egg except for young pups. The white on its own is, I think, quite acceptable.

It is a mistake to give a dog very large breakfasts to try and alter a weight problem. The main meal at night is the best one for altering weight, either up or down. The high protein versions of the expanded food that you would use for racing dogs are not supposed to need meat, but when the dogs are getting a lot of work and a lot of racing about $1\frac{1}{2}$ lbs (675 g) of meat is the usual amount added to the soaked meal. There is no need to feed vegetables with this type of food because all the vitamins that they would get from vegetables are already in the preparation. The meat can be cooked or given raw. It's not a bad idea to cook a bit of tasty meat to make some decent soup to finish soaking your meal with and to then give the dogs some raw and some cooked.

When feeding the old-fashioned way a good wheatmeal should be used together with some brown bread to form the basis of your feed. Vegetables such as leeks, celery, nettles (these are excellent and contain a great deal of iron), apples and carrots can then be cooked, minced and mixed with the meal. Retain the vegetable water for use in soup. Do not mince the carrots: they are very indigestible and come out more or less in the same form as they went in. If you want to use them, cut them up and cook them with the other vegetables so their goodness will be in the water, then throw the carrots away.

Most meals require soaking for a fair time until they are soft and have swelled to capacity; this is very important with the expanded variety. It is also important not to feed them too dry; fluid is a vital part of the racing dog's intake.

To this mixture you add your meat. As stated, about $1\frac{1}{2}$ lbs (675 g) is a good guide but the quantity should be determined by the size of the dog and the amount of work that he is doing.

When you wish to either remove or put on weight, the cereal content is the one to adjust. There are times when dogs are very hard to get weight off. It's no good simply cutting the food down – the dog then feels starved and if he is in training you run the risk of weakening him. White fish, making sure that all the little bones are removed, or chicken

Geoffrey de Mulder's kennel range.

are good sources of protein and carry less fat than red meat. Any meat that you use should be fed raw and all the fat removed. In extreme cases the cereal can be substituted with broad bran to make up the bulk. Bran has absolutely no food value at all, but it fills the dog up and satisfies his appetite. It also keeps his bowels working. Naturally it can't be fed dry and whatever you use to wet it with must contain no fat at all. Vegetable water is as good as anything, and a few vegetables, mainly greens, can be fed as well.

Most large racing kennels have a set of scales so their dogs can be weighed every day after their afternoon exercise. This is done at this time of day because they have emptied their breakfast on the afternoon walk and you get a true weight. When you have a dog in a very important race he should be weighed before breakfast; the morning weight is always about 1 lb (500 g) or so up, so you can then work out what the evening weight is going to be and adjust your breakfast accordingly. Dogs fed late after racing seem to be up in weight the next day but by the following night that has been naturally adjusted.

Somebody with just one or two dogs is not going to want the expense of a set of platform scales, but quite a good idea is to make friends with the local railway station and mostly they will let you use theirs occasionally. The schooling tracks where you go for private trials will probably have a set and let you weigh your dog.

Weight is very important in training. By knowing the weight of your Greyhound when he races and comparing times sensibly you can establish his best racing weight and try and feed him to keep that weight correct. This is not easy and takes some practice but eventually you get it right.

Cramp can be an awful problem in Greyhounds. It has quite a lot to do with feeding, though it is not always related. The main problem is too much protein, so one of the first things is to cut the dog's protein intake. If feeding one of the high protein expanded foods you can change to a lower protein one of the same make and take care not to increase the amount of meat that you are already using. This method can be tried but it is not infallible. There are various pills on the market for this problem and the names and where to obtain them will be found in Appendix B. Extra vitamin E and C are a help in cases of cramp, but when all else fails it is wise to take advice from your veterinary surgeon.

Grooming has a very important part to play in the training of racing dogs. It doesn't just keep them clean – although that matters too and reduces the problem of fleas to a great extent: the point of grooming is really to massage the muscles and this can best be done with your hands. Starting at the front of the dog work your way from the shoulders and neck down the back to the hips and hindquarters.

There are various makes of rubbing oils on the market, details of which can be found in Appendix C. They serve to clean your dog and for the most part warm up the muscles while you are rubbing them in. Try not to be too heavy-handed when massaging and avoid using your thumbs on the hindquarters as this seems to remove the hair and you finish up with a partly bald dog. This looks terrible and it's an awful job to get the hair to grow again. Too much rubbing can be worse than no rubbing at all. The muscles should always remain flexible; don't get them as hard as iron as this leads to cramping and quite often to muscle injuries. In your grooming kit you should have a good pair of body brushes – the ones made for horses are the best. They are expensive but, if looked after, will last for years. You will also require a pair of grooming gloves, a good flea comb, a tooth scraper, a medium tooth brush, some good toothpaste, peroxide, olive oil, cotton wool, cotton buds for cleaning the ears, a clean towel and, if you are able to get

them, a pair of rubber brushes since these are better than the rubber gloves.

(OPPOSITE)
George Curtis
grooming.

A bottle of methylated spirit is useful for cleaning scurf. If applied on a pad of cotton wool and rubbed firmly over the dog, it cleans up a lot of surface dirt and loosens any scurf from the coat, which can then be brushed out. Always use plastic bottles and containers, especially in the kennel. They won't break so easily and broken glass is a disaster when it splinters onto the kennel floor. However hard you try, a small sliver of glass may be left after the clearing up and if it ends up in a dog's foot it can cause really serious problems.

A Greyhound's teeth need cleaning every day. The reason is very simple. They are fed on soft food all the time and this seems to cause tartar to form on the teeth. Use the toothpaste on the brush and put a drop of peroxide in the water that you wet the brush with. The scraper is only necessary occasionally or if a dog comes to you with very bad teeth that the brush won't touch. If the teeth are left uncleaned

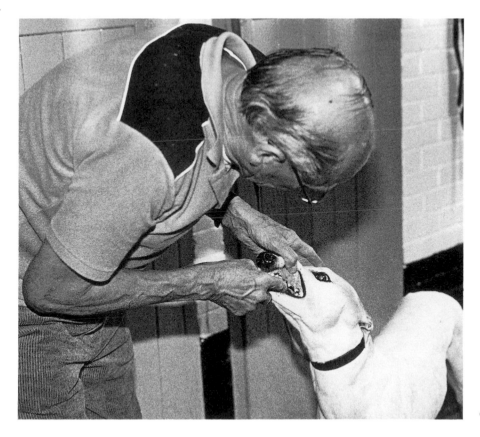

Cleaning a dog's teeth.

eventually the tartar builds up and rots them, and then the bad teeth have to be removed. Quite apart from the health hazard there is nothing worse than taking your dog to the races and he opens his mouth to show everyone two jaws full of filthy teeth! The asides about your kennel management will be unprintable.

Ears need cleaning quite often, hence the cotton buds in your kit. Dip the bud in a tiny drop of olive oil and *gently* go round the inside of the ear, removing the wax and dust deposits. Don't use too much oil otherwise more dust will stick to it. Wipe the ear out with a clean piece of cotton wool when you have finished.

Having rubbed your dog with oils which will loosen all the dead hair that is ready to come out, you then comb him with the flea comb. This will remove the old hair and also any flea dirt as well as the odd flea. It's amazing how much dirt one flea will produce. Every dog has some kind of a flea problem, particularly in the summer, but it can be kept under control. Other ways of doing this will be discussed later on. The rubber brushes in your kit are excellent for removing dead hair.

The body brushes now come into use, partly to clean the dog and partly to massage the muscles. It is a good idea to use one on each hand and get a good rhythm going. It's very difficult to explain exactly how to do this so all the grooming exercises are illustrated. Strapping with the brushes should take from five to ten minutes and should be done lightly but firmly. After this polish your dog off with the clean towel.

I have an electric grooming machine made by Flextol. It is very good because it cleans the dog at the same time as massaging him with the rotating brush. Unfortunately Flextol have stopped production of the machine made only for dogs. They do, however, make the same machine in a larger version intended for horses. Looking at the information sheet I think it would be quite suitable for Greyhounds. The information on this can be found in Appendix C.

When this part of the grooming is finished your dog can be offered a little olive oil; most dogs love it and will lick it out of your hand. A dessertspoonful is about the right amount. It is very good for their coats and feeding it has other advantages as well – helping the digestion is one. The dogs get to look forward to this part of their grooming session and it can be regarded as a kind of treat; it is much better for them than chocolate drops.

Feet are terribly important and should be examined every day. The day after a race day the feet should be washed in warm soapy water with a drop of disinfectant (Dettol or Savlon) in it. An old toothbrush is as good as anything for brushing round the quicks and removing any

dirt or sand. Dry them off well and then inspect them for any small abrasions or cuts, particularly in the palm of the foot.

Using the electric groomer – most dogs love it!

Sand sores in that part of the foot can be very painful and if not treated at once can result in a kind of wart that has to be poulticed and then squeezed out when it has come to a head, leaving quite a large hole that then has to be treated as well. This can keep the dog off the track for some weeks. Prevention is better than cure with this kind of problem. Hints about how to help this condition are given in the section on minor injuries (p. 45).

One of the most important items in your grooming kit is a good pair of nail clippers. There are quite a few designs available so choose the one that you feel suits you best. The clippers must be sharp otherwise they simply tear the nails and leave jagged ends. I also keep a few emery boards in my kit; they are useful for rounding off the nail when you have cut them.

The most usual way to cut nails is to have the dog standing on the floor, and to pick one foot up at a time. Personally I lie them down on a table since I find that far easier for both me and the dog (see illustration). Remember that it is very important not to cut the quick. With light-coloured nails the quick can be seen and it is therefore easy to avoid a mistake. When the nails are black it is rather harder, so the best thing to do is to cut as far as you dare and then finish off with the emery board. Nails need to be quite short for two main reasons. The first is that if they are too long and you are running on a grass track, they dig in, and if they happen to get stuck the result is quite often a pulled ligament in the toe or what we call a 'knocked up toe'. The second reason is that if you leave the nails like talons it can cause spike marks and scrapes on other dogs if they happen to strike into them on a bend.

The amount of exercise that you give your Greyhound is determined largely by what races you have planned for him.

I was very pleased to be able to discuss exercising and fitness with Lilah Shennan, one of the most experienced coursing trainers around today. She soon dispelled the myth that coursing dogs have to be walked about ten miles a day! Her dogs do about three to four miles on the road. As she pointed out, you take your life in your hands on the roads today, and the fumes from cars and lorries are extremely bad for the dogs.

However, she gallops the dogs and she has an uphill gallop. Galloping uphill requires more effort from the dog and develops the drive muscles in the back and hindquarters derived from the pushing action, as it would in the shoulders from the pulling action.

If your dog is getting plenty of racing, say, two runs a week or perhaps three a fortnight, then I feel that one gallop in between is quite enough. If you do gallop your dogs you must have somewhere safe to do it. It's easy enough for them to get injured on the track without getting injured at home.

If you are getting a dog fit to win one particular race it's not a bad idea to go to a safe schooling track and have a trial; this would also be sensible if the dog was not getting enough runs. Try to take him to the right type of hare. It's no use having a trial on an inside hare if your race is on the outside hare because your dog will probably miss his break.

Many trainers I know, when getting their dogs ready for a race, will

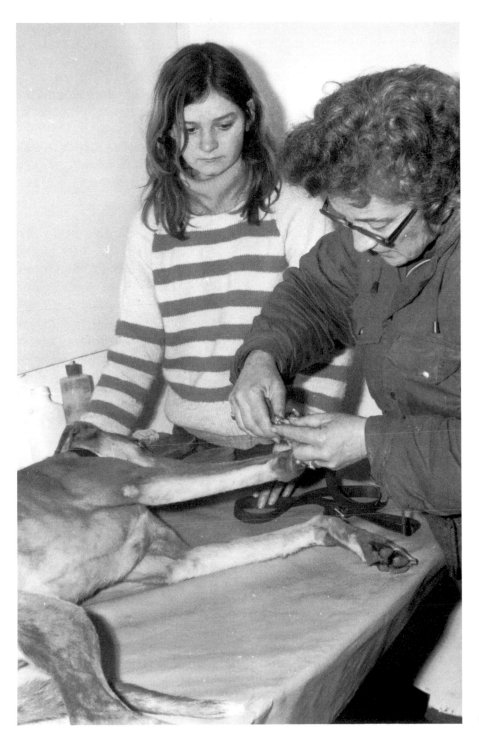

Cutting a dog's nails.

take a dog whose form is consistent at the race track and give it a trial, making a careful note of its time. This way they can get a guide on times between the track they race at and the schooling track. This is a great help when getting a dog ready to win a race because you can work out to within a few 'spots' on the clock the time that your dog might be expected to do in the race – barring accidents and bad luck, of course.

Walking, once your dog is fit, is merely an exercise for him to take the air and have a change of scenery. So, instead of bashing the roads, a nice walk round a wood, field or park, if you live in town, is the best, and not too far at that.

The expression 'leaving your race on the road' is in some cases very apt. On race days, for instance, I would vary the routine to a small extent. Keep to your times but instead of walking for an hour I would cut that to twenty minutes, and the same in the afternoon. Grooming can still be done but don't rub the dog to death; don't do anything that will tire or take the freshness off your dog.

Feeding on race days can be kept to the normal routine as much as possible; give the same breakfast, in any case. I give a very small racing feed at about 3.30 in the afternoon. This consists of a pinch of meat, white of an egg, dessertspoonful of glucose and a drop of soup. This serves to take the wind off the dog's stomach and having had something he does not spend the rest of the evening fretting for his food.

I would like to mention walking machines. Many people think that they are useless and that the dogs hate them. If they are used incorrectly that is quite true. But they have their uses and the main one, to my mind, is that when you have a very bad spell of weather in the winter, if all your dogs are taught to walk on the machine, they can still get their walking without getting frozen to death or soaking wet, and their feet cut to ribbons on the ice.

Another good thing in their favour is that they can be used for walking dogs that have been lame. Naturally you would put your dog out first to empty himself properly before going on the machine, but the beauty of it is that the dogs *have* to walk, and I mean walk at a certain speed which can be adjusted to suit your programme. It helps to build up their muscles after a lay-off and in some part speeds up the time that it takes to get dogs back on the track.

There are double and single machines and if you happen to possess one it is a good thing to teach as many dogs as you can to walk on it, so that when you need the facility the dogs know the score. Some dogs take to this very easily and others require a great deal of patience. It is

(OPPOSITE)
Geoffrey de Mulder's gallops.

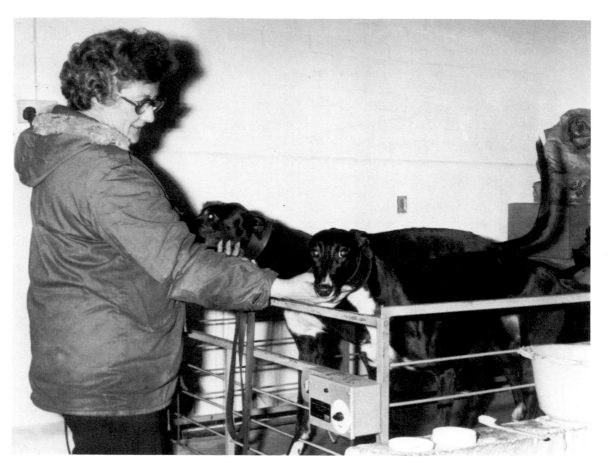

Two happy dogs on the walking machine.

necessary to have the dog's collar quite tight and tie the lead firmly to the front bar thereby leaving you both hands free to hold the collar and encourage your dog. Whatever you do, don't let the dog slip off the back of the machine; apart from the injuries he might sustain it will frighten him and then you will never win. At the least sign of real trouble, turn it off. Never ever leave a dog on a walking machine alone or when you are out of reach of the stop button. Having said all this, there is really no substitute for a good walk in the fields or woods so the dogs can enjoy the sun and fresh air, see a rabbit or two and have a sniff in the hedgerows, even if you have to load them up in the car to get there.

Talking of cars, a word of warning: all vehicles can be quite lethal in the summer in the hot weather. When you go to a trial or race meeting, particularly during the day, park your vehicle in the shade if you can. If you can't, then leave the back or the doors open and try to keep the vehicle cool. There have been some dreadful accidents involving Greyhounds, caused by nothing more than heat stroke.

After a dog has had a run, in the hot weather particularly, for a short time his temperature will go up, as high as 105°F (40°C), and it has to be brought down pretty rapidly. Many people simply don't think and they shove the dogs into a hot vehicle and perhaps go away, leaving the windows open, to watch the next race or trial or have a gossip with a friend. It takes less than half an hour to kill a Greyhound from heat stroke.

What needs to be done first is to sponge your dog all over with cold water. Then, if you have finished your job, don't stand around chatting but drive away with all the windows down and try to get a good draught through the car. Whatever happens, don't shut the windows until the dogs have stopped blowing.

If you are going to put your dog back in a kennel and the weather is hot, keep him out until he has cooled down; many of the track kennels can be very hot and airless. I suppose this is not really the fault of the management – they have to give priority to security and that cuts down the space allowed for ventilation.

Remember, if a dog dies from heat stroke in the way I have described, you have only yourself to blame. It is sheer carelessness.

5 Health and Welfare

Minor injuries and kennel management

These are many and varied and, like 'bad pennies', always turning up. Some we bring upon ourselves through carelessness and bad management, others appear through no fault of our own.

FLEA CONTROL

In the winter this is not the problem that it can be in the summer; fleas don't seem to breed in the winter and you get only the odd one here and there (unless you happen to have central heating in the kennels, in which environment they will breed). However, in the summer – and some summers appear to be worse than others – if you don't keep a careful eye on your dogs the whole thing can become completely out of control.

There are many preparations on the market, most of them very expensive. I use Nuvan Top and a preparation called Duramitex. The latter costs only a few shillings and is actually designed for pigeons, but it works well and can be bought at most pet shops. Nuvan Top is obtainable from the vet. The same manufacturer makes another spray called Nuvan Staykil, which is only for use on the beds and never on the dogs. The beds can be kept clean by changing the bedding every week, sweeping off all the dust, etc., and then spraying the Staykil in the corners before putting down the clean bedding.

I have had dogs arrive at the kennels with the fleas literally dropping off them. Never allow a dog to enter your kennels with fleas on him. This is the quickest way to spread them all round the kennel and once they get in it's very hard to get rid of them. One method of killing fleas quickly is to bath the dog in a good insecticidal shampoo and repeat at the specified intervals until the problem is cleared. This kills the fleas stone dead. Flea collars are both popular and effective but always be sure that you either use them with dogs in single kennels or with dogs

(OPPOSITE)
Westmead Cannon, winner of the 1986 British Breeders Forum.

that are quiet and do not play about in the kennel. They are very dangerous if eaten, so never use them on puppies because they tend to pull them off one another and chew them. Always remove them if you have a dog that is off-colour (it does in fact advise this on the box).

A good flea comb and careful grooming avoids most of this problem.

TICKS

These can be picked up from paper, wood shavings, sheep, or from the grass in the summer, and are not very common. Dogs coming from Ireland always need picking over as they tend to carry them mainly due to the Irish system of allowing pups to run about on farms, where they pick up sheep ticks.

It's no use just squashing them; you have to pull the head out and then squash them. The best way is to put a drop of ordinary paraffin on them, which will loosen the head and they then are easy to remove.

Look between the toes; if a dog is carrying ticks you will be astonished at how many are in the feet. Some manufacturers claim that their flea collars will kill ticks but I have never found them to be very effective.

It is important to be sure to remove the head of the tick; if left in the skin it can cause an infected sore.

WORM CONTROL

This is very important. Keep your dogs clean, inside and out, and you will cut down many problems. I have heard a lot of people say, 'I don't worm my dogs until I want to win a race with them; it improves their performance enormously.' To me that is quite ridiculous; why waste good food feeding the dog and the worms? Some worms go hand in hand with fleas, so you can give yourself a double problem.

Worms cause instability in a dog's weight – it tends to go up and down; they cause bad breath and dry, staring coats, so what is the point in leaving them there?

There are various types of worms, the life cycles of which are described in the following pages. There are countless pills to eradicate the different kinds and it is advisable to take your veterinary surgeon's guidance on which preparation to use.

Many Greyhound people still use Garlico. It is not very easy to get now because Freemans, who used to manufacture it, went out of business. A very similar preparation is now available, and is made in Ireland. It's all right in small doses for freshening up a dog but it does not kill the worms; it merely purges a few of them out, leaving the heads in to develop again. A waste of time in the long term.

ROUND WORMS (*Toxacara canis*)

Roundworms are a very common problem in pups. Adult worms in the intestines shed eggs that are passed in the motions. Larvae moult within the egg and become infective about four weeks after being passed. Eggs taken in by the pups develop into adult worms in the intestines.

Eggs taken in by adults mostly migrate into the muscles and don't develop into adults. In dogs a few do develop in the intestines but even fewer do this in bitches.

In pregnant bitches the larvae in the muscles become active and migrate across the placentae to infect pups before birth. Visceral larvae migrains can be a problem in humans, especially children, so routine worming, especially of pups, is important.

HOOK WORMS (*Uncinaria stenocephala*)

These are not very common but do occur, especially in Greyhound kennels. Adult worms in the intestines shed eggs which are passed in the motions. Infection is mainly by the oral route but larvae can also migrate across the skin. Pre-natal infection can occur as in *Toxacara*.

Larvae survive best in damp conditions, so keep runs dry and clean out daily to control infection. Earth runs may act as a persistent source of infection.

Pre-patent period, i.e. interval from infection to production of eggs in motion: fifteen days.

TAPEWORMS (*Dipylidium caninum*)

These are very common (not controlled by Panacur). Adult worms live in the intestines. Segments containing eggs are passed with the motions or move out of the anus of their own accord, causing irritation. The segments are eaten by adult lice or by larval fleas and develop to cysticeroid in louse or flea (intermediate hosts) in about thirty days. If the intermediate host is eaten by a dog the cysticeroid develops into an adult worm in the intestine. Pre-patent period: two to three weeks.

To treat it is necessary not only to kill the worms but also to control external parasites.

TAPEWORMS (*Taenia hydatigena*)

Adult worms live in the intestines and segments are passed in the motions or separately. Intermediate hosts: sheep, cattle and pigs. Cysticeroids develop on peritoneal surfaces, especially on the omentum.

Infection of dogs can be prevented by thorough cooking of any offal fed, and the cycle broken by not allowing access of the intermediate hosts to dog faeces.

TAPEWORMS (*Taenia multiceps*)
Adult worms live in the intestines and segments are passed in the motions or separately. Intermediate hosts: sheep. Cysticeroid develops in central nervous system, causing 'gid' or 'sturdy'.

Don't feed brains or spinal cord nor whole sheep's head or vertebral column unless fully cooked.

TAPEWORMS (*Taenia ovis*)
Adult worms live in the intestines and segments are passed in the motions or separately. Intermediate hosts: sheep. Cysticeroid develops in muscle so thoroughly cook all mutton and lamb to prevent infection.

TAPEWORMS (*Taenia pisiformis*)
Adult worms live in the intestines and segments are passed in the motions or separately. Intermediate hosts: rabbits. Cysticeroid develops in the muscle. Always feed rabbit cooked.

ALL TAPEWORMS
Cysticeroids take two to three months to develop in intermediate hosts. Pre-patent period: six to eight weeks. Little risk to humans but observe hygiene as (rarely) can develop to cysts in humans.

TAPEWORMS (*Echinococcus granulosus*)
A particular problem in some rural areas, especially Wales. Relatively difficult to treat, needing larger doses of anthelmintics. Adult worms live in the intestines and segments are passed in the motions or separately. Intermediate hosts: herbivores. Cysticeroid develops anywhere in body. Cook meat thoroughly. Can cause hydatidosis in humans ingesting eggs.

MANGE
There are two main types of mange that you are likely to come across:

Sarcoptic Mange
This type is very contagious and spreads through the kennel in no time at all. It can be picked up from dirty bedding, mainly straw that's been lying around, or more easily from other dogs. The treatment is varied;

years ago we used to use a mixture of sulphur and rape oil, which was quite effective but extremely messy. Benzol Benzoate, Cooper's Mange Dressing, Alucan and Tetmosol are all very good and can be obtained from the vet. Whatever happens, don't ignore it because if you do one morning you will find that the dog is red raw all over and nearly nude!

Demodectic Mange

This is fairly rare, luckily, as it is sometimes impossible to get rid of. Some dogs are born with it and in some it develops. In the early stages the hair drops off around the eyes and on the ears and the skin looks dry and slightly scaly. You will have to take the vet's advice with this and there are now preparations that you can use. At one time it was a killer and there was no cure.

QUICKS

These are always a problem, particularly nowadays with all the sand tracks. Some sand seems to be worse than others, so if your track happens to be one of the bad ones you will need to be extra vigilant about washing your dog's feet and checking them every day. Prevention is better than cure with this problem, so never, if you can help it, let them get sore. There are quite a few preparations on the market that can be applied, the names of which will be found in Appendix C.

A good general rule is to soak your dog's feet in a solution of Epsom salts the day after the race, making sure that you have removed every grain of dirt. Dry them well and then have a good look round them, wiping them out again with cotton wool soaked in peroxide. This has the effect of fizzing out any little bits of dirt that might be left and it also tends to draw the quick into the nail. Calamine lotion is quite good for doing this as well.

When you are unlucky and you have a dog with very bad quicks that split, then the only way is to poultice them with Animalintex, and this has to be done every day until they are better. Each time you remove the poultice wipe the quicks out with either surgical spirit or peroxide. Some people soak them every day but I think that this tends to make the foot very soft and prone to further damage.

It's not a bad idea to put Vaseline around the quicks before you run on sand. As long as you wash the feet in nice warm water after the race the sand will come out with the Vaseline, and this definitely saves the quicks some damage.

An old-fashioned idea that still works and costs nothing is to ask your butcher for the contents of his pickling pot when he changes the pickle. The saltpetre and fat in the water make for a very good soaking solution.

SAND BURNS

These are little or large cuts in the palm of the foot, quite often caused by tiny bits of shale in the sand, or indeed by excessive running. They are mainly found on the hind feet and can be a real problem because they are very sore and keep the dogs off the track, sometimes for weeks. Here, again, prevention is better than cure and a little Vaseline smeared in the dog's foot just before he runs often works wonders. Zinc and castor oil cream is good also for this problem. Any injuries that come under the heading of cuts in the foot can mean serious trouble. I have tried stitching the cuts but no matter how long you leave the stitches in they always split open again and you are back where you started. I understand that some vets are now cutting back the appropriate web, which then takes pressure off the palm of the foot and prevents the continual splitting of the cut. This, however, would be a matter for your vet and the earlier this injury is taken to him the less time your dog will spend off the track.

Minor sand burns can usually be cleared up with a good washing in surgical spirit or peroxide every day and then dressing with a good healing ointment such as zinc and castor oil, Padsanol, or Copo Quick ointment. Another method is to paint them with ordinary creosote using a child's paint brush. They are, however, a condition that cannot be ignored.

Under this heading also come the very odd wart-like growths that appear in various places in the dog's foot. In my opinion they are the result of a grain of sand getting under the skin of the foot and then nature taking a hand and setting up a counter reaction, like an oyster does in making a pearl. These have to be left until they are fairly prominent then soaked in quite hot water to soften the surface and, with the dog on the table, squeezed. I am afraid that it is quite painful for the dog but there seems to be no other way. You will find that lots of little bits come out, looking rather like a cauliflower, and you must get all the matter out, even if it takes two or three days with the intervening time spent poulticing. Once it's all out the foot will bleed a little. Wash it out well and put some antiseptic powder in the hole. Keep a bandage on for a couple of days, by which time it is normally on the mend.

NAILS

The most usual injuries with nails are that they get broken or pulled out. If they are pulled right out, leaving just a small hole, this can be cleaned and dressed with Terramycin spray (a can of this is a very useful addition to the medical chest). Keep the wound bandaged until it has dried up and is no longer sore.

With this type of injury, if you find any swelling in the toe which persists despite poulticing, go to your vet and have an X-ray of the toe, because it may mean that the bone in the toe is damaged.

Quite often the nail is not completely pulled out and part of the shell is left, with a tiny bit of quick inside the nail. The best thing to do in these cases is to ask your vet to cut off the nail level with the toe. Eventually the nail grows again.

EARS

Greyhounds are not a breed that is prone to canker of the ear. I have, however, come across the odd case, mostly caused by dirt. In the advanced stages canker causes a smelly discharge, but in a mild case you would notice the smell only when you are cleaning out the ears, and you might also notice the dog scratching at his ear. Your vet will give you some drops to put in the ear and, if caught in the early stages, this condition soon clears up.

Ear flaps can get torn very easily, either in fights or on a sharp object. This happened to one of my dogs – I'm Slippy – at the start of the 1983 Derby. He stuck his head in a blackthorn bush while out on the walk and tore the inside of his ear from end to end. Luckily, I live only two miles from the well-known Greyhound vet, Paddy Sweeney. He stitched the ear for me and we went into the first round of the Derby with twenty-two stitches in Slippy's ear. I might add that I nearly went into a decline over the whole affair and I didn't dare tell the owner until his dog had won his first round. John Quinn, Slippy's owner, was very good about it; he merely went white and said, 'My word, you are a cool cookie!'

KENNEL SICKNESS

There seem to be quite a few permutations of this complaint! Mostly the dog is sick and refuses food and this normally lasts for twenty-four to thirty-six hours. Do not offer any food for twenty-four hours but some rehydration water can be offered in small amounts. Do not allow a lot to be drunk at one time and withhold totally if drinking results in vomiting. A few packets of salts such as Lectade should always be kept in the medicine chest and your vet will supply you with this. After twenty-four hours your dog will be looking for food, so a light feed, fish or chicken, would be suitable. If this stays down then you have no problems. Do not offer food if it is not wanted.

Sometimes the dog is sick and has diarrhoea as well. Provided there is no blood in the diarrhoea or the vomit, withholding food for twenty-four hours is best but, again, the rehydration water can be offered. Giving food in cases like these merely feeds the bug. The vet will give you some medicine for this problem to keep in your medicine chest so follow the instructions. If it is a normal kennel sickness it should be clear in forty-eight hours.

If there is any blood in the diarrhoea or vomit call your vet straight away. Don't wait for a day before you call him. This could be a serious enteritis or even Parvo virus. Don't take the dog to the surgery, but ask for a visit. It could be a very contagious problem and you would merely spread it around by taking the dog off your premises. It does help to stem the spread of kennel sickness if the dogs affected are not allowed out of the kennel until they are clear. This might take four days. Some might say that you can't keep a dog in for that length of time, but you can and I do. It can stop the bug spreading to a great extent and keeps dogs in more or less controlled conditions as regards temperature.

Persistent vomiting with no diarrhoea requires attention from your vet. It could mean that the dog has picked up something which is causing irritation in the stomach or an obstruction of the intestines.

TONSILLITIS

This is quite common in large kennels. It is a bacterial infection and can therefore be treated with antibiotics with some success. The glands at the top of the throat swell up and can quite easily be felt by feeling the neck below the ears (see illustration), or the tonsils can be seen by looking down the dog's throat. In some cases the dog goes off his food simply, I think, because it hurts him to swallow, and he will often have a throaty cough as well. Get your vet's advice on the best antibiotic to administer.

COUGH

Coughs are quite common and very catching. They may be viral or bacterial and therefore may not respond to antibiotics. If antibiotics are prescribed it is to combat the secondary infections, which in the case of viral infections are mainly congestion of the lungs and/or bronchitis.

There are some inoculations that you can give the dogs for this

(OPPOSITE)
Tonsillitis looking
down the throat and
feeling for glands in
the throat.

complaint, but they are expensive and not always effective. Should you wish to use one of these it is necessary to consult your vet.

URINATION

Some dogs, mainly older ones, have trouble with their water-works and will take a very long time to urinate – they stand there doing little drips and spurts. This problem can often be cleared up by giving them one Hexamine a day for a week and at the same time feeding some cooked pearl barley. This should be well boiled and the water strained off. It can then be mixed with milk at breakfast and used as soup for the evening feed. This will normally clear the condition but if it doesn't then you will have to seek your vet's advice.

ANAL GLANDS

These need squeezing out occasionally. They are situated on either side of the anus, and when dogs are not fed hard food, such as bones, they tend to become blocked. Your vet will show you how to clean them out – it is quite a smelly job! The main sign of this problem is the dog chewing at the base of his tail.

TAR ON THE FEET

This is only a problem in the summer when the weather is hot and you happen to be walking your dog on the road. It does not occur only on roads that have been freshly tarred; sometimes when the weather has been very hot it melts the tar on all the roads. The best solution is to try and avoid it, but, failing that, rub the feet with lard and keep on rubbing until it comes off. It will eventually, and this is the only way that I know that works. Washing is a waste of time; the water simply sets it.

BROKEN TAILS

(OPPOSITE)
Healing a broken tail.
(A) The dark mark in the middle indicates a fracture or dislocation.
(B) Plastic hose pipe.
(C) Plastic hose pipe cut horizontally and warmed in hot water to make pliable.
continued on page 52

You won't come across these very often but when you do, they are a pest. If the tail is broken very high up you will have to bandage it firmly and then cover it with Elastoplast. Be careful not to do it so tightly as to stop the circulation or you might finish up with no tail at all. The most usual place for a break is either the middle or towards the end. If there is no open wound there is no need to bandage. An open wound should be dressed and covered with a light bandage. Then take a piece of plastic hosepipe, long enough to leave about 2 ins (50 mm) on either side of the break. Slit it down one side, soak it in very hot water so that it becomes pliable, open the slit and fix it round

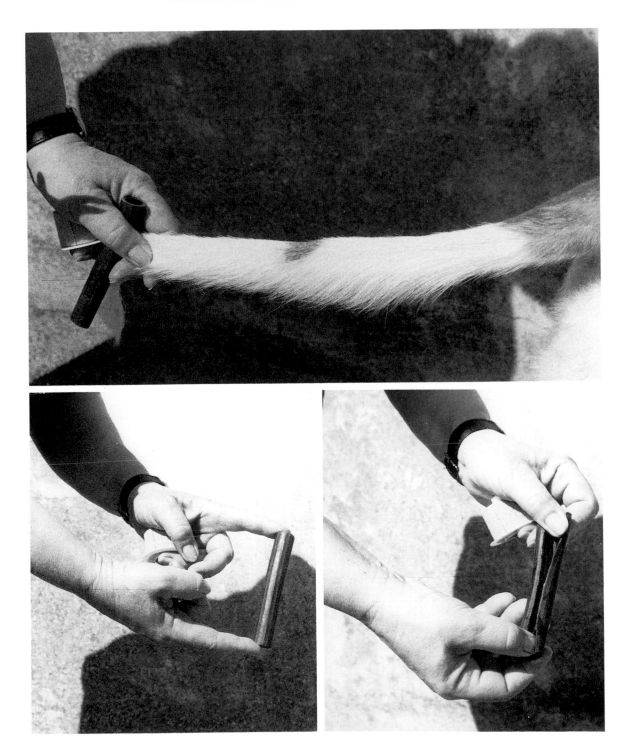

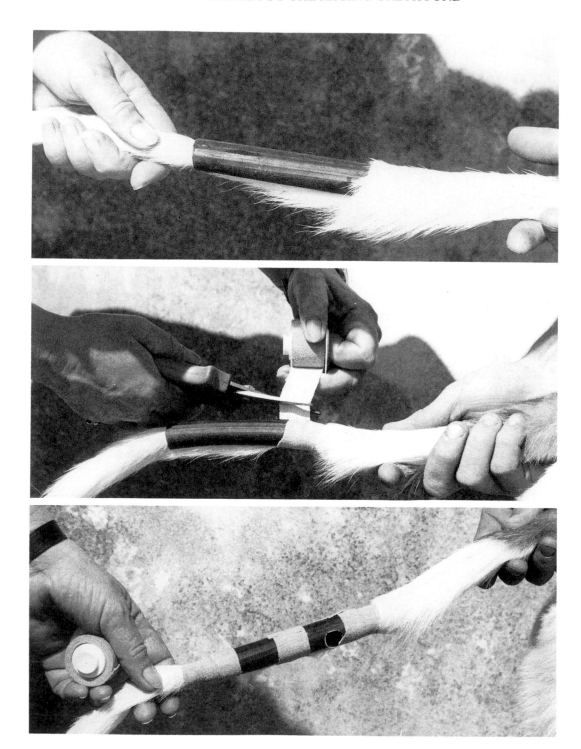

the tail like a splint. Tape it with sticky tape at either end so that it does not slip, leaving the middle piece open so that air can get in (see illustration). After about two weeks the tail joint should be healed.

TAIL ENDS

These are a real curse, and it is mostly because the dog is happy and wags his tail that they occur. Wrap cotton wool and wound powder round the end and fix in place with plaster. Do be sure that you change the plaster about every three days otherwise the end of the tail can go rotten. If you have a very persistent problem one way is to pad the edge of the bed, because that is normally the place where the damage is done. A sack filled with straw and fixed to the bed front works quite well, and the walls can be protected in the same way. It does not look very pretty but then damaged tail ends look even worse. In some very extreme cases the end of the tail has to be amputated, and that, of course, has to be dealt with by your vet. However, with reasonable care and some forethought this can usually be avoided.

WOUNDS AND CUTS

Clean wounds and cuts with salt water, making sure that you have removed all the dirt, and then dress with an antiseptic powder. Leave them open where you can and they will heal very quickly. If they do require a bandage be sure that it is changed every day. Don't let the dog lick his wounds; it merely encourages infections. The best way to prevent licking is for your dog to wear a box muzzle for a few days.

Pettifer's Green Oils, although considered very old fashioned by many people, have some useful properties and can be used on small wounds with great success. They are, I believe, very good for sand burns as well.

A good disinfectant to have in your kennel medicine chest is either Milton or Eusol. Never use them neat; always dilute according to the instructions.

SPLIT WEBS

Very often you find what I call 'little nicks' in the centre web on either of the front feet. They are a nuisance, to put it mildly. I quite often put some drying agent on, such as wound powder or Terramycin spray, and when I run the dog again I push in a good smear of Vaseline or zinc and castor oil cream between the toe. The main cause of the injury is the dog scraping the bars of the traps. The cream or Vaseline causes a reduction in friction and quite often works. On the other hand, some

(OPPOSITE)
(D) Fitted onto the tail over the fracture.
(E) Plastering both ends.
(F) The finished result.

dogs split the web well back without any help from us. In this instance, whatever happens do not let the web grow together again. Wash well and pack between the undamaged toes with dry cotton wool, then soak a good wad of cotton wool in some whisky (no, the dog won't get drunk from the fumes), put this piece between the damaged web and then bandage nicely. Remove the bandage every day and repeat the performance. After about ten days you will find that the edges of the split have healed up well. Leave your dog off the track for about three weeks and when you take him back pack the web well with Vaseline. It's a bit radical but I have found it very effective. On the other hand, there are some cases where the 'little nicks' gradually worsen and in the end, to make a clean job, it is necessary to have your vet cut the web back and stitch up either side. Depending on how fast it heals you should be able to run the dog about fourteen days after the stitches are removed.

The best bandages for foot work are either Johnson's conforming bandages or cling bandages. They stretch easily and go round the corners so you don't have great folds of bandage to cope with.

CORNS

These occur in the pads of *any* foot – they are not fussy. In my opinion it is a waste of time and money having them cut out; they always grow again. Soften the pad first with cream and keep it covered, then try some good corn plasters or Freezone liquid corn remover. These remedies sometimes work, but not always. There are dogs who have a permanent corn problem which can only be kept under control by constant paring, and even then they are lame on a hard surface.

There are some herbal pills that can be used and Pam has had great success with these. The stockists are listed in Appendix C.

BLOOD IN THE URINE

If this occurs after your dog has raced, more particularly in the hot weather, it is due to over-exertion causing muscle damage and staining of the urine with muscle pigments, or to the rupture of small blood vessels in the urinary tract. It can be a bit frightening the first time you notice it. Make a point of washing your dog down in cold water; using a sponge douse him thoroughly all over. He will steam himself dry in about five minutes, then be sure to put a jacket on the dog to prevent any chilling. Some dogs are more prone to this than others but if once the dog has done this always wash him down in cold water, winter or summer.

If the condition continues into the next day or if the blood looks very bright you must seek expert help straight away.

MUSCLE LAMENESS AND GENERAL LAMENESS

It's jolly difficult sometimes to know where a dog is lame. We know the animal is lame but on occasions it can be very hard to pinpoint the exact cause. A great many wrongs stem from a fault in the dog's spine, and I believe that it is a good thing to take your dog to an osteopath. There are quite a few who now treat dogs and do so very successfully; there is also a clinic in the Midlands that specialises in laser treatment for bone injuries and muscles. The names and telephone numbers of some of these people can be found in Appendix C.

There are also various machines marketed for muscle therapy. The Medtron Stimsonic unit is one such machine. It combines faradic stimulation with ultrasound and either treatment can be used independently. The faradic muscle stimulator has its own head which is used solely for moving the muscles from the motor points to help with tracking down which area of the dog is injured.

When the faradic head is used, the dog must be well soaked in water around the area to be stimulated and the head needs to be left in the water for about five minutes so that the chamois leather covering and little sponges underneath are completely saturated. All dogs vary in their reaction to muscle stimulation and it is necessary to establish at what level a good contraction can be obtained on each dog. To find soreness on your dog, gradually increase the output on an area of the dog that you feel sure is normal, until you get contractions that are comfortable for the dog. When you have established the correct setting then use the head in the area where you feel the problem lies. Upon contraction of the sore or torn muscle you will get a fairly loud reaction from your patient.

It should be understood that you will get a reaction if you hit one of the nerves. The location of these nerves should be studied and professional advice sought before starting to use this section of the machine. It is essential to use your stimulator the day following a race if you think you have a problem. In fact it is quite a good idea to do this as the norm and go over your dog entirely; this helps to remove any stiffness that might be present after a hard race.

The ultrasound head must be used with a good coupling gel, which is obtainable from the makers of the machine. The ultrasound head must not be left on unless it is either in use with the coupling gel on the dog or immersed in water, otherwise it will overheat. It is therefore

The muscles of a dog.

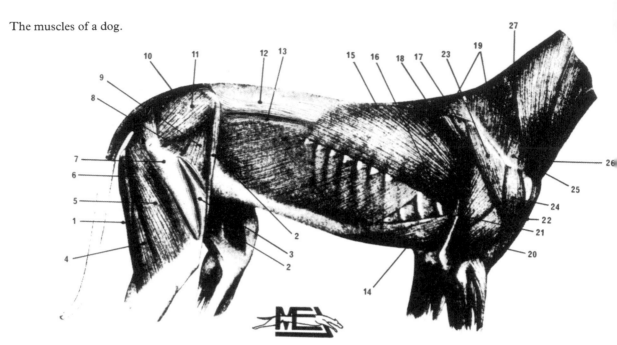

NO.	MUSCLE NAME	MUSCLE ACTION	NO.	MUSCLE NAME	MUSCLE ACTION
1	GRACILIS	Extends hip and hock joints-controls sideways movement of hindlegs.	14	DEEP PECTORAL	Extends the shoulder joint, draws the body forward and the leg backwards.
2	SARTORIUS (Whip Muscle)	Flexes hip and draws leg forward.	15	LONGISSIMUS DORSI Thoracic Portion	Extends spinal column - raises front and rear ends of the spine.
3	RECTUS FEMORIS Portion of Quadriceps Femoris	Extends stifle.	16	LATISSIMUS DORSI	Supports the front leg - draws the leg backwards and closer to the body.
4	BICEPS FEMORIS lower portion and Semimembranosus	Extends hip, stifle and hock when racing but flexes stifle when patient lying on side.	17	INFRASPINATUS	Flexes or extends the shoulder joint.
5	BICEPS FEMORIS upper portion	Extends hip, stifle and hock when racing but flexes stifle when patient lying on side.	18	Portion of TRICEPS Muscle	Extends the elbow joint when shoulder blade is fixed.
6	SEMITENDINOSUS	Extends hip, stifle and hock when racing but flexes stifle when patient lying on side.	19	TRAPEZIUS Cervical and Thoracic Portions	Raises the leg and draws it forward.
7	LATERAL VASTUS	Extends stifle.	20	TRICEPS Lateral Head	Extends the elbow joint when shoulder blade is fixed.
8	TENSOR FASCIA LATA Rear Portion	Flexes hip and extends stifle.	21	TRICEPS Long Head	Extends the elbow joint when shoulder blade is fixed.
9	TENSOR FASCIA LATA Front Portion	Flexes hip and extends stifle.	22	BRACHIOCEPHALIC Lower Portion	Draws leg forward and fixes or flexes neck.
10	SACROCOCCYGEAL	Raises and moves tail sideways.	23	DELTOID Upper Portion	Flexes shoulder joints and raises elbow
11	GLUTEAL MUSCLES	Extends·the hip joint.	24	DELTOID Lower Portion	Flexes shoulder joint and raises elbow
12	LONGISSIMUS DORSI Lumbar Portion	Extends spinal column - raises front and rear ends of the spine.	25	OMOTRANSVERSE	Helps extend the leg.
13	PSOAS MUSCLE and QUADRATUS LUMBORUM	Holds spinal vertebrae steady and flexes spine or hip joint.	26	BRACHIOCEPHALIC Upper Portion	Draws the leg forward and fixes or flexes·the neck.
	G E T T O K N O W Y O U R D O G		27	SERRATUS Cervical Portion	Moves shoulder backwards and forwards during leg movement.

essential to have a good layer of gel on the dog when using this head for treatment. Airspace between the head and the dog will cause overheating of the head and discomfort to the dog. Tissue burns can occur if the covering of gel is not sufficient. The head should always be kept moving over the area being treated; the higher the output, the faster the movement. Periosteal pain and overheating can occur if the output is too high and the head is not moving fast enough over the area being treated. Any signs of distress from the dog mean that the output level is too high and it should be reduced until the dog is comfortable.

The continuous ultrasound is used primarily as a healing agent. When the sore points have been located it is very important to know the extent of the injury before embarking on a course of treatment. Therefore some expert help, either from your vet or an osteopath, should be sought and his or her advice taken. Experience with ultrasound has shown that it is most effective if the dose is increased over a period. The correct format might vary from four to eight minutes, three times a day, allowing at least four hours between each treatment. Treatment levels are recommended by the makers. However, the faradic head can be used to ascertain whether there is any pain remaining in the area being treated. When all the pain has gone you can be almost sure that you have cracked it. However, it might be wise to continue treatment for, say, another two days.

When treating an area near a bone with very little muscle covering, it is essential that you use the pulsed ultrasound. Toes and wrists are prime examples of this. To my mind, it is best to treat these under water. Put the dog's foot in a bucket of tepid water, bringing the level over the wrist or the toe; as water is such a good conductor of soundwaves there is no need to use the gel. The head should be held in the water about $\frac{1}{2}$ in. (12 mm) away from the area being treated and the level can be increased by 1 watt on the lower scale.

The type of ultrasound treatment that I have always considered very effective is the combined output. With this treatment you are able to stimulate the muscle whilst applying the ultrasound. It increases the blood flow to the muscle and removes any congealed clots and waste fluids from the area, which in turn speeds up the healing process. This is done by using the ultrasonic head, together with the passive electrode, round the dog's girth.

The stimulation level is set below the stimulation point of the dog and the surge button turned on. You can vary the surge, thereby controlling the muscle contractions. During this part of the treatment the ultrasound level is as for the normal treatment.

The gel which conducts both ultrasound and electrical currents must be used for combined therapy on the target area and the passive electrode should be well soaked with water when applied to the dog's girth. More information on this machine can be found in Appendix C.

Sand tracks seem to produce a great many niggling muscle injuries, mainly in the hips and shoulders. The use of sand surfaces has reduced the number of toe and hock injuries, but it seems to have increased wrist, back and shoulder injuries.

A recent innovation in the equipment used for treating lameness in Greyhounds is magnetic field therapy. I have no direct experience of these machines but I understand that it makes the dogs very tired for the day of the treatment; also I am told that some sections of the Greyhound fraternity are using this as a slowing agent when they don't want their dogs to win. However, every man has his own ideas about what is right and wrong. More information on the MFT system can be found in Appendix C.

The Rollax a Mite machine, marketed by the Therapy Advisory Service, seems a very comprehensive massaging unit. It is very easy to use and can in no way damage the dog. Further details can be found in Appendix C.

Although I have talked about muscle lameness in this section of minor injuries, some muscle injuries are very serious and cannot be repaired. Vets specialising in Greyhound care do operate on and repair badly torn muscles and ligaments, but the success rate is, I am afraid, very variable.

TENDONS

The majority of tendon injuries are sited at the back of the metacarpal bones below the wrist. They are more common in the front legs but can also occur on the hind ones. You will find a swelling and discolouration underneath the skin (bruising), caused by the rupture of the tendon sheath and the subsequent bleeding.

The treatments are many and varied. Some people advocate cutting the tendon, which works, but I am afraid it sometimes leads to the next tendon rupturing. Some Greyhound vets have been achieving quite a good success rate with laser treatment. In any event the first thing to do is to hose the tendon and follow that up with ice-packs. Ice-packs need a bit of ingenuity to prepare. I find that the leg of an old pair of tights works very well. Stuff the ice down the leg and then crush it so that it is almost flat, then wrap the ice-pack round the leg, bandaging firmly. Don't worry about the bandage being too tight – it soon loosens up when the ice melts. This treatment must continue until the bruising and inflammation have gone, then you can take the dog to the vet and see what he advises. The vet is not able to do anything until you have first reduced the inflammation. During this time the dog should have absolutely no exercise whatever.

In the old days, before anyone thought of cutting the tendon, we used to poultice the area for about a week and then soak it in vinegar and saltpetre for about two weeks. This was a time-consuming job as we had to keep changing the dressings and re-soaking them, but it was quite amazing how the tendon hardened and healed. There was always a lump there afterwards but, on the whole, once the tendon had hardened there was rarely any more trouble.

We used to use this treatment with knocked-up toes as well, and while it produced a bigger toe as a result, it was as hard as iron and never went again. The only problem is that the joint becomes immobile.

Injury to the tendon at the back of the leg, above the wrist, is quite another matter and requires veterinary attention. Such cases are pretty hopeless, though. They can be fired, although that is considered rather old-fashioned now. I think that they have tried carbonfibre treatment, and I would imagine the laser has been used – with what success I don't know.

When tendons are cut the important thing is to walk the dog – in fact it is essential – and I begin that therapy even before the stitches come out.

In all muscle injuries the thing to remember is: try not to be impatient. A lot of people do not rest their dogs for long enough. Walking is essential after a lay-off to get the muscles working again and to strengthen them. Running them too soon merely aggravates what is already a weakness, and in many cases the lameness occurs again.

The other type of exercise that is most beneficial for after-care in Greyhounds, or in any lame dogs for that matter, is swimming. To start with, the distance that they swim has to be carefully controlled as it is very strenuous. In order to swim dogs have to use all the muscles in their body, just as we humans do. So 50–100 yds (50–100 m) is plenty, or about 3 minutes. Pam has a lake near her kennels and the dogs go for their swim behind a rowing boat. Horse-swimming complexes are great if there is one anywhere nearby and the owners will let you use it. These have a raised platform in the middle and a ramp down to the water. One stands on the platform and the dogs swim round. It's as well to have plastic collars on a piece of nylon lead

or rope as the dye in leather collars sometimes runs out onto the dog. Whatever you do, don't use any type of slip lead or slip chain because if the dog happens to struggle the slip tightens and cuts off the air supply – very dangerous.

On the other hand, if you happen to live near the sea, that is wonderful. Wear a good pair of waders and take the dogs in on the lead – they love it. There is no need to go very far out; the water should be deep enough when it's approaching the top of the waders! Sea-water has all sorts of minerals in it and it is accepted that it does the dogs a great deal of good.

As with everything else moderation is the key word, and the dogs get to really enjoy swimming if they are introduced to it properly.

PARVO VIRUS

Due to the very stringent regulations regarding inoculations imposed (quite rightly) by the National Greyhound Racing Club there are very few incidents of this disease among dogs of racing age. However, it is essential to have all puppies (dogs from eight weeks to fourteen months) properly inoculated. Unfortunately the virus is endemic in all towns in Great Britain and there is not much that can be done about it. Eventually I suppose that, like distemper and hard pad, it will be more or less eradicated as the level of immunity in the dog population rises. At the moment, however, every puppy that is born is at risk after the age of six to eight weeks, which is when the immunity that they get from their mother's colostrum (milk that the bitch produces during the first twenty-four hours after the birth of her litter) begins to wane. Provided that the pups are not subjected to a very severe challenge from the virus at this crucial age the usual regime of inoculations suggested by your vet should give them the protection they need. I feel it is a good thing also to give them a Parvo booster at twenty weeks, and then a full booster at thirteen to fourteen months.

To start with, when you are considering mating your bitch, give her a full booster just before she comes in season. Don't wait until after she is mated to do it. There have been cases where the pups have been born dead or the bitch has aborted, and this has been put down to being injected with the booster while actually in whelp. Always have it done before she is mated and in plenty of time. This practice helps to boost the immunity that she passes on to the pups.

It is as well to try and keep the pups away from other dogs and from too many visitors while they are at the high-risk age. The reason for this is that other dogs carry the virus on their feet or on their coats,

(OPPOSITE) Swimming.

and while they are immune they can spread it around. People outside the family, and even the family, can do the same thing. When you go to race meetings and visit the kennels there always make sure that you change your shoes and clothes and wash your hands before going in to the pups. You cannot be too careful, but the foregoing are commonsense precautions.

Actually Greyhounds are not among the breeds that seem to suffer most from this virus. Rottweilers, Dobermans and Dalmatians are some of the more susceptible breeds, according to research recently undertaken by Intervet whilst they were developing their new vaccine.

Let's assume that you have a litter of pups that might be at risk. The first thing you will notice is that one of the pups doesn't eat up as well as usual. It might sit by itself, and I have noticed that the day before it actually goes down with Parvo, the pup becomes snappy and bad-tempered with the others. That puppy wants watching very carefully. It is sometimes difficult to catch the pup actually being sick, which is the real sign that something is wrong, but if you spot one that is unhappy and definitely off its food, separate it from the others and put it on newspaper, which can later be burnt. If and when the puppy is sick, it will vomit a frothy kind of slime, either yellow or white. After this *do not* (and I must emphasise this) give him any food or drink. It merely makes him more sick, and every time that happens he will lose not only what you have given him but also some of his own body fluid as well. The greatest single killer with Parvo, apart from the virus itself, is dehydration.

It is now time to call your vet with all speed, for the puppy will need a drip and something to stop it being sick. Most vets don't like taking pups with Parvo into their surgery as it is very contagious. Unless the pup is either vomiting blood or has bloody diarrhoea, your vet will probably give a sodium chloride and dextrose drip into a vein, and perhaps inject 0.25 cc of Acepromazine (or ACP for short) combined with an antibiotic straight into the bloodstream. The ACP will help sedate the pup for a bit and relax the stomach muscles, which then stops the sickness for a time.

In some very severe cases puppies start producing blood from both ends almost at once and then it is essential for them to have a plasma expander such as Haemacel. This has to be put into the vein by your vet. A dextrose drip can be put under the skin and the more, within reason, that you can give the pup the better. Your vet (if you show some common sense and willingness to help) will provide you with the drip, the giving set and a needle. When giving a dextrose solution

(OPPOSITE)
Westmead Move, winner of the 1986 John Power Grand Prix.

under the skin the first place to start is the scruff of the neck, where you will have a bit of loose skin. Put your needle, correctly connected to the giving set which is of course turned off, under the skin at a flat angle. Don't dig it in or when you turn the drip on you will find that it won't run properly. Let the solution flow in at a steady rate, fairly fast but not actually pouring. Probably 100 ml at a time would be about right. Rub the lump of fluid gently when you have finished to help it disperse. With any pups that I have to drip feed I do this at least three times a day and my vet calls once a day to give whatever is necessary into the vein. It is not wise to try and drip into the vein yourself because with pups it can be very difficult to raise the vein enough for an inexperienced person to get the needle in the right place, the vein then gets riddled with holes leading to further complications. The more dehydrated the pup becomes, the flatter his veins and it is only too easy to go straight through them.

It is a very stressful time for both you and the pup, or pups if you have more than one with Parvo at the same time. Generally if one contracts it some of the others will as well and it is pretty exhausting having three or four pups to drip feed three or four times a day. By the end of about two weeks you will be beginning to feel absolutely dreadful but each morning that they are still alive gives you hope for the next day and you carry on. It is largely a question of pure determination and patience. I know only too well that you can't save them all, and that those you lose very often die of clinical shock. But pups have been on drips for up to three weeks and have eventually grown up into strong healthy specimens with a special quality about them, which stems from the time they were dying but had the will to live.

People will tell you that the affected pups will be no good, but this is not strictly true. If the after-care that you give them is good and you feed all the right supplements to save their bone there is no reason at all why they cannot grow up and run just like any other Greyhound. In fact it has been proved that they can. At one time there was a lot of talk that it affected their hearts, but I believe it has been established that the pups have to be subjected to a very strong challenge from the virus before they are three weeks old for this to happen; most now have maternal immunity at this age so this syndrome is rarely seen. It was very common when the disease first appeared and at that time there was no maternal immunity. These pups showed no sign of illness at the time but died of heart failure later.

When you reach the stage that the pups have stopped being sick, start them on a little Lectade, which is rehydration water, a teaspoonful at a time, every hour perhaps. If that stays down for a day you can think about some solids. Whiskas rabbit or chicken, a little at a time, seems to be easily digested and does not strain their stomachs. Keep on with the rehydration water but *do not* give them any milk for quite some days. Milk seems to start the diarrhoea off again and with their insides in such a delicate state you can be put back to square one. Raw mince, very lean, usually follows on quite well and then some brown bread with a little gravy added to it. Once you are over these first days of the pups eating carry on adding a bit at a time until you get their digestion stabilised.

Ask your vet for advice on what to give to help their bone. I had occasion to be interested in a very bad case not long ago and the vet gave them some Petcal. This worked very well and the pup grew up with lovely strong straight bones after being so weak that when it first went out it would fall over in a breeze. The important thing whenever you have a problem and you need your vet's help is to try and get him or her on your side. It's no good telling vets what to do – it merely puts their back up.

Fractures in the Racing Greyhound (Written by Jeanne Jones MRCVS)

The racing Greyhound is an athlete and the breaking of a bone can be the worst thing that can happen to it. Races are won or lost by as little as hundredths of a second, and injuries of any kind, particularly fractures, slow the dogs down considerably. Unless displaced fragments can be replaced so that there is little or no deviation from the norm, the Greyhound will not race again so efficiently.

Even a minor deviation from normal, however small, can interfere with the working of the muscles which are attached to the bone. Happily, thanks to modern science and technology, fractures are not always as disappointing as they could be.

Fractures can appear as smashed bones, clean breaks or slivers of bone pulled away by the ligaments attached to the bone. Roughening of the bone surface can cause pain and wear and tear of the tendons running over the rough surface, and a callous or bony lump can interfere with the flexing of the joints. The tendons running over the lump or callous appear to be shortened as they have further to travel over the callous and this can cause bunching of the toes, for example. In reverse,

FIG. 3 Bones and
joints of the
dog.

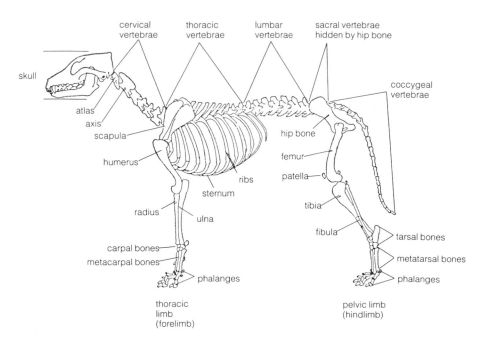

cervical vertebrae
thoracic vertebrae
lumbar vertebrae
sacral vertebrae hidden by hip bone
skull
coccygeal vertebrae
atlas
axis
scapula
hip bone
humerus
femur
ribs
patella
sternum
radius
tibia
ulna
fibula
carpal bones
tarsal bones
metacarpal bones
metatarsal bones
phalanges
phalanges
thoracic limb (forelimb)
pelvic limb (hindlimb)

Half skeleton of dog

tendons damaged or cut in the foot cause the lengthening of the toe so that a flat toe is produced.

According to the position of the break the Greyhound may or may not race again. Fractures which occur near joints or which impinge on them are usually more serious than those occurring in mid-shaft, although once again this depends upon the bone fractured. A further consideration in assessing the practicality of bone repair in a racing dog is the short racing life of a Greyhound. It is of little use repairing a bad fracture if the dog is not good enough for stud, is not suitable for a pet, or would be too slow or too old to race when he has recovered.

FIG. 4 The pelvis. The illustration on page 68 shows the various positions for plates and screws depending on the fracture.

It is not kind, therefore, to repair fractures where the Greyhound cannot race again, has no pet home to go to and is unsuitable for stud. There is little point in allowing a dog to suffer the pain and trauma of a fracture repair and then put him to sleep at the end of the treatment for one of the above reasons. This may sound hard but each injury must be assessed individually according to its severity and the circumstances surrounding the animal at the time. Kindness must take paramount importance in all the decisions affecting that dog.

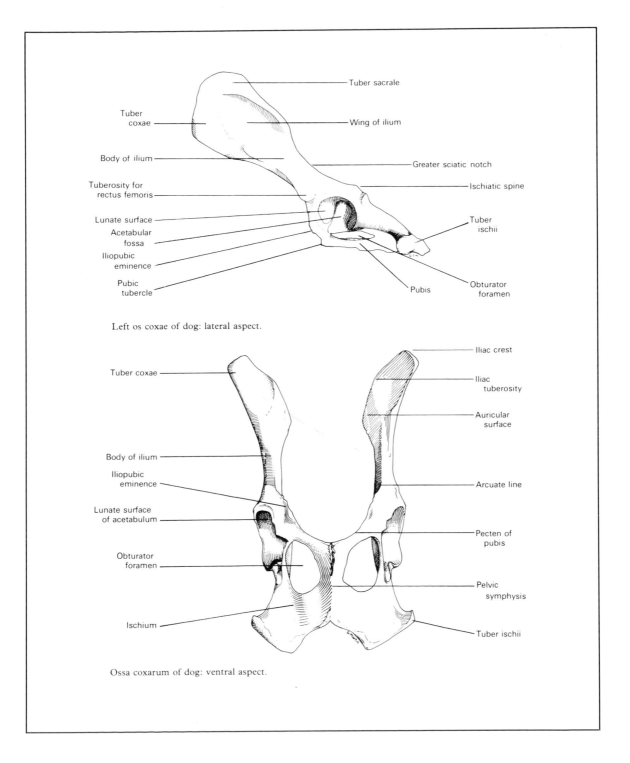

Left os coxae of dog: lateral aspect.

Ossa coxarum of dog: ventral aspect.

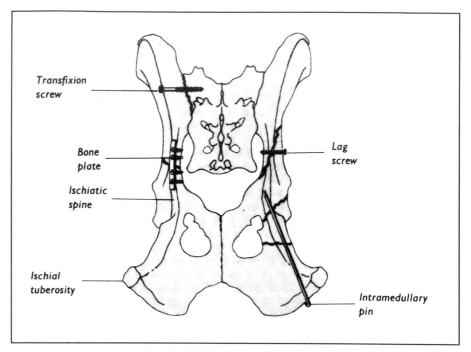

Fractures to the pelvis are rare and usually caused by a collision between the animal and the rails. Animals suffering fractures involving either the pelvis or the hip joint are most unlikely to race again and unless they can be successfully retired they should be put to sleep. Dislocations of the hip joint can be relocated and, if they are returned fairly promptly and there is no damage to the bone structure, the dog can race again; rarely does the dislocation reoccur.

Fractures of the pelvis proper, depending on the location and severity, can be repaired with plates, pins or wires. It must be realised, however, that in order to reach the bone the muscle mass covering the bone has to be cut and dissected away from the fracture site, relocated and sutured together at the end of the fracture repair. This process obviously impairs the action of the muscles thereby slowing the dog or making him unsuitable for racing.

As with fractures of the hip socket, a fracture to the head of the femur which provides the ball of this ball-and-socket joint, is bad news, the usual result being permanent lameness. A fracture in the shaft of the femur, on the other hand, depending on its actual form, can be repaired with plates and screws or pins. However, the only person who can decide this is the veterinary surgeon who is actually doing the operation because no two fractures are exactly alike and when bones break the resulting trauma can involve muscles, nerves and blood vessels.

Injuries to the stifle joint involve four major bones – the distal end of the femur, the patella, the tibia and the fibula – and are usually very serious and, except in the case of puppies when avulsion of the tibial epiphysis can sometimes be successfully treated, older dogs rarely race again. Tibial fractures are usually plated.

Hock fractures are common racing injuries and the outcome depends on which bone is involved. There are seven in the hock, and according to the severity of the displacement, the dog may or may not race again. Fractures of the scaphoid bones usually repair very well while those involving the os calcis are not so successfully treated. Fractures of bones in the lower row of the tarsus usually involve more than one fracture and fragmentation of the part of the bone at the back of the

X-ray showing complete dislocation of the hock.

Fracture of the scaphoid bone, top row tarsal bones.

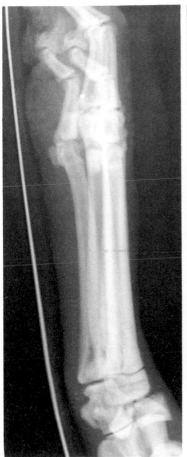
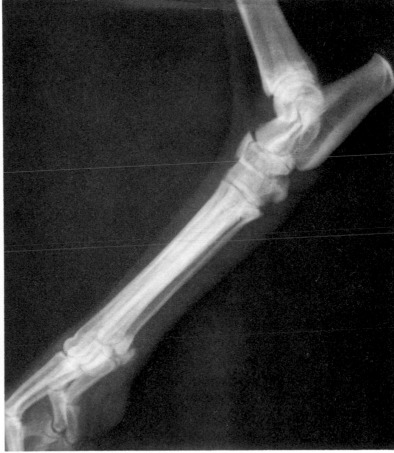

hock. These can be very difficult to deal with and can result in collapse of the hock with deformity and lameness. Dislocations of the hock also occur.

Fractures of the metatarsus can be dealt with by pins or plates, but sometimes the best results, when only one or two bones are involved,

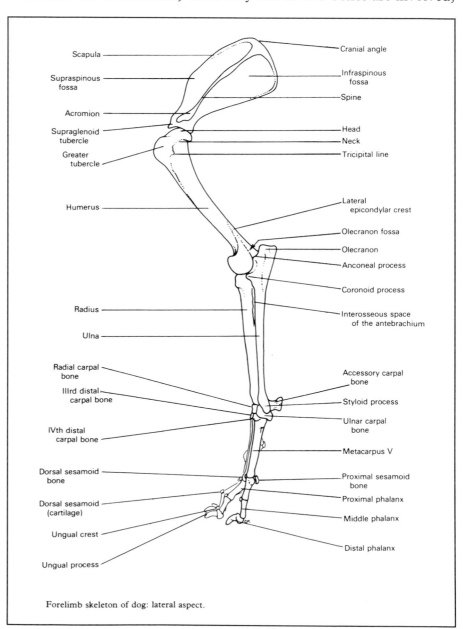

Scapula

Supraspinous
fossa

Acromion

Supraglenoid
tubercle

Greater
tubercle

Humerus

Radius

Ulna

Radial carpal
bone

IIIrd distal
carpal bone

IVth distal
carpal bone

Dorsal sesamoid
bone

Dorsal sesamoid
(cartilage)

Ungual crest

Ungual process

Cranial angle

Infraspinous
fossa

Spine

Head

Neck

Tricipital line

Lateral
epicondylar crest

Olecranon fossa

Olecranon

Anconeal process

Coronoid process

Interosseous space
of the antebrachium

Accessory carpal
bone

Styloid process

Ulnar carpal
bone

Metacarpus V

Proximal sesamoid
bone

Proximal phalanx

Middle phalanx

Distal phalanx

Forelimb skeleton of dog: lateral aspect.

FIG. 5 Fore limbs and hind limbs of the dog.

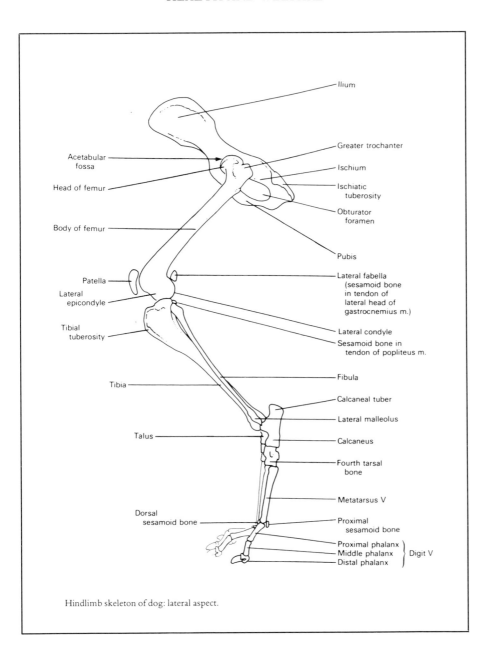

Ilium

Greater trochanter

Acetabular fossa

Ischium

Ischiatic tuberosity

Head of femur

Obturator foramen

Body of femur

Pubis

Patella

Lateral fabella
(sesamoid bone
in tendon of
lateral head of
gastrocnemius m.)

Lateral epicondyle

Tibial tuberosity

Lateral condyle

Sesamoid bone in
tendon of popliteus m.

Fibula

Tibia

Calcaneal tuber

Lateral malleolus

Talus

Calcaneus

Fourth tarsal bone

Metatarsus V

Dorsal sesamoid bone

Proximal sesamoid bone

Proximal phalanx
Middle phalanx
Distal phalanx

Digit V

Hindlimb skeleton of dog: lateral aspect.

will be seen by straightening the broken bones and bandaging the paw using the sound bones as splints.

Fractures of the sesamoid bones sometimes occur and can be treated by the removal of the pieces of broken bone and applying a cast to the foot. The bones will callous, the only problem being that sometimes the callous spreads too far and fuses the bones together resulting in pain after racing and eventually arthritis.

Fractures of the toes or digits can be dealt with by pinning, plating, screwing, or bandaging as in the metatarsal repair. Minute pieces of

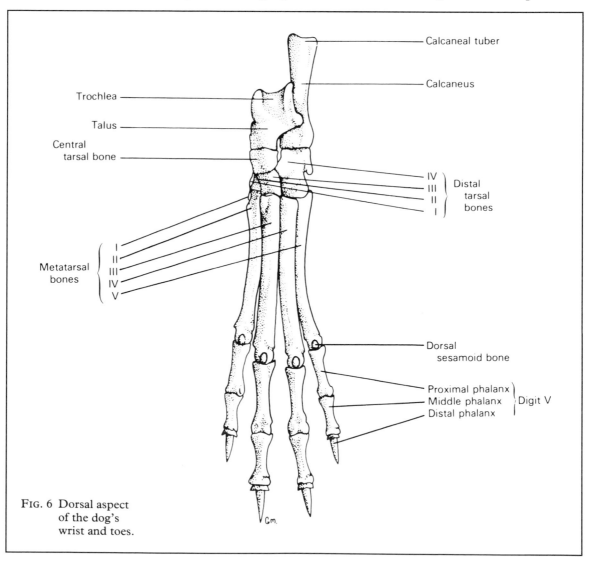

FIG. 6 Dorsal aspect of the dog's wrist and toes.

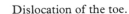

Dislocation of the toe.

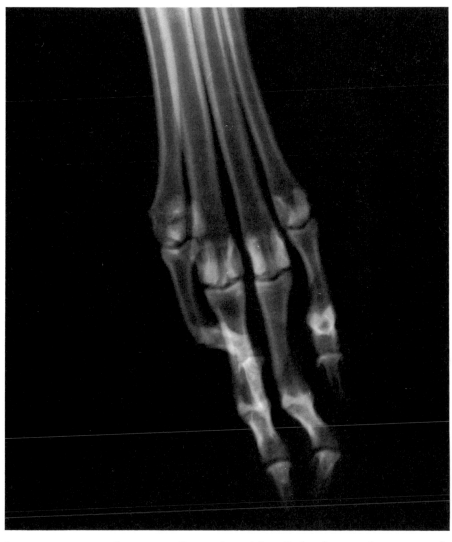

bone are very often torn from the side of the bone when a toe is dislocated, together with part of the periostium. This happens when the insertion of the tendon is subjected to too much pressure. If toes are very badly fractured or dislocated they may be removed. Removal of toes is obviously the last resort, since the remaining digits will be at much greater risk. Greyhounds with more than one toe missing are not raceable.

It must be realised that the extent of any fracture injury does not end with the severity of the bone damage. On fracture, the bone can rupture nerves and blood vessels, it can puncture the surrounding tissues and skin and can protrude to the outside to become contaminated with debris and bacteria. Fractures which occur near the joints or which impinge on them are usually more serious than those occurring in mid-shaft because of the almost inevitability of arthritis attacking the joint at a later stage.

Fractures in the shoulder region directly due to a racing injury are rare and usually due to a collision with a fence. Fractures of the scapula are very rare indeed. More frequent are injuries to the humerus, radius or ulna and these can be either mid-shaft breaks or epiphyscal fractures involving the joints. All can be repaired with the use of screws, plates or pins. There is, however, a further hazard in fractures in this area: damage to the radial nerve, a branch of which lies just under the skin, can cause paralysis of the leg.

The brachial plexus, which lies in the axilla or armpit region and supplies the nerves of the foreleg, can, if damaged, also result in paralysis of the limb.

The wrist has seven bones present, three in the top row and four in

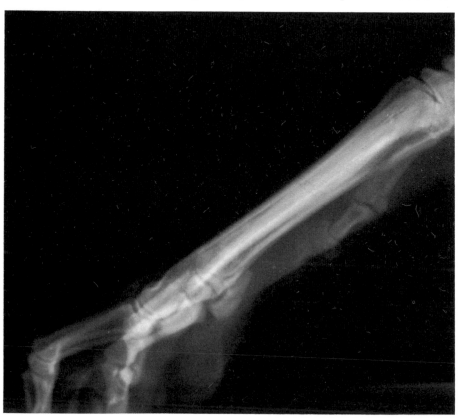

Fracture of the acessory cardal or pisiform bone.

the lower. The most common fracture which occurs here is the one involving the accessory carpal or pisiform bone. This can be an outright fracture or just a chip taken off by the pulling of the attached ligaments. Chips are usually removed, while fractures may be repaired by wiring or screwing. Sometimes these repairs give good results while at other times they are unsuccessful and arthritis may follow. Injuries to the wrist are the worst of the common racing injuries to treat as lameness all too often reoccurs in spite of treatment.

Fractures of the metacarpus and digits or toes of the forelimb are much the same as those of the metatarsus and the hind digits, but injury is more common in the fore leg, particularly toe sprain and fractures of the digits.

Physiotherapy

Physiotherapy is the science of treating disease by physical means, such as light, heat, cold, electricity etc. We have all used physiotherapy in one form or another, albeit unknowingly, e.g. cold water on a sprain or warmth to help an ache.

The common methods in use today include ultrasound, infra-red heat, magnetic field therapy, faradism, whirlpool therapy, laser and short wave radio therapy. Each form of physiotherapy is useful in some context and can be complementary to another. Equally, if used in the wrong way it could do considerable harm.

FARADISM
This is useful for restoring function to muscles which have not been used because, for instance, a leg has been broken and in plaster. When the break is healed faradism can be used but it should never be applied on fresh or unhealed fractures. Faradism can be used to help muscles where the nervous control has been damaged. It can also be useful to break down adhesions following muscle injury.

INFRA-RED HEAT
This is useful in mild injuries to relieve pain and increase the circulation. It is used quite frequently by most trainers for strained shoulders and hind muscles.

ULTRASOUND THERAPY
This increases the blood supply to the injured part, enhances the cell metabolism and thus heals the injury more quickly. Care must be taken

to use the correct setting as periosteal damage can occur to bones when the frequencies are incorrect.

MAGNETIC FIELD THERAPY

This is one of the newest forms of treatment available. It increases the blood supply and the activity of the cells by positioning a magnetic field on the injured surface of the muscle. MFT is also useful for healing fractures. Once again, the settings must be right as incorrect settings can exacerbate injuries by increasing inflammation. MFT is also used for 'toning up' a dog, but too long a session can cause the dog to be so tired following the treatment that he races well below his best.

SHORT-WAVE RADIO THERAPY

This has gone out of favour as it interferes with television reception. It was useful for sprained wrists and follow-up treatment for fractures, also as a heat treatment for muscle injuries.

LASER THERAPY

This is the most recent type of therapy. A cold laser is used; the infra-red is the best available and the type I find the most useful. It can be used for healing superficial wounds, muscle injuries, helping to heal injured wrists as well as for treating fractures to 'speed up' healing and prevent arthritis. The penetration of the laser is from 3–6 cms ($1\frac{1}{4}$–$2\frac{1}{2}$ ins) depending on the model of machine used. This, of course, means that for very deep injuries the penetration power may not be sufficient. The injury must be pin-pointed as the covering power of most lasers is not more than 3–4 cms ($1\frac{1}{4}$–$1\frac{1}{2}$ ins) in diameter.

Laser treatment has revolutionised the treatment of fractured hocks in Greyhounds. Previously even fractured scaphoids could lose up to half a second in time over 525 yds (475 m). Now they scarcely lose time at all. Fractures in the lower row of tarsals are not so successfully treated but even these respond to some extent to laser therapy.

WHIRLPOOL BATHS

These are useful to freshen up tired animals, say, between heats and finals of races. They can also massage muscles which are bruised. Most dogs like them and relax. After the first whirlpool bath the dog usually looks forward to enjoying the next when he realises that one is on the cards.

All of the machines mentioned above are expensive and very few trainers would possess all of them, or, even owning them, would have the time or the skill to use them. Trainers and owners of machines should take the time and trouble to find out how to use them properly and make sure that the manufacturer's recommendations and settings are followed. Improperly used machines can do more harm than good to the dog.

The cheapest form of physiotherapy available is also the most neglected: cold water and ice-packs. If more of these were used as emergency measures on acute injuries the damage to be repaired by the veterinary surgeon or physiotherapist would be much reduced.

6   Breeding

I am sure that most people will agree that the choice of your brood bitch is one, if not the most, important part of your breeding programme. In my opinion far too many Greyhound bitches are used for breeding that are totally unsuitable for some of the following reasons.

The first is size. It is unwise to breed from a bitch that is very small – they don't make good broods and, generally speaking, have small puppies. The size of the puppies seems in part to be determined by the size of the mother. I feel that a bitch needs to be at least 58 lbs (26 kg) in weight to be any good for breeding.

The second point is temperament. Very highly strung or nervous bitches are quite useless for breeding. These traits are hereditary and always come out in the puppies. I hate to say this but many of the pups from a widely used and very popular dog now standing in Ireland are coming out very nervous indeed. It would be interesting to try and trace that fault in the breeding – it must be somewhere – but then again he is producing some very fast dogs. I think that Greyhound breeders have a tendency to breed for speed, or so they hope, regardless of any recessive faults the line may have. This, to my mind, is why the choice of bitch is so important.

The third point to consider is never to breed from a bitch with an obvious genetic fault, such as an incorrect bite or badly deformed jaw. Puppies never do well with that burden to carry as it affects their capacity for feeding, making them slow, and while they are in the litter the competition is usually such that they get left behind in the 'food stakes' and their growth suffers as a result.

These three points are the obvious ones. Many people will pooh-pooh them and say that they have known bitches with all these faults breed a perfectly good litter. Maybe, but don't forget that 'one swallow does not make a summer' and that by breeding from bitches, or dogs for that matter, carrying genetic faults you are simply moving them on again to the next generation. I know that I shall be unpopular for

Lone Wolf (4) beats Low Sail to win the 1986 St Leger.

saying this but I believe that within Greyhound breeding a great deal of 'culling' needs to be done. Unfortunately it takes so long to get puppies on the track that by the time it comes to breeding everyone has forgotten what the parents were like and what sort of puppies they produced, unless of course they were very famous sires or dams.

To 'cull' successfully one has to know intimately the antecedents and the progeny of the animals that you are proposing to use. This is fairly easy with show stock who reach maturity far earlier than racing Greyhounds, are bred from earlier and whose antecedents with their faults and virtues can be seen back at least three generations.

So where do we go from there? Well, the only thing to do is to avoid the glaring pitfalls and try to research your proposed parents as far as you possibly can. Another point that I should like to make here, and for which I shall probably be hung, drawn and quartered, is that when choosing your bitch don't fall into the trap of breeding from one who managed to win the first race at the local track and is a charming character and family pet. Keep her as the family pet and love her dearly to the end of her days, but, at the same time, get your economic act together and realise that to embark on breeding a litter costs an astronomical sum today. We shall be talking about the bloodlines in the English and Irish dogs in a later section and trying to outline some of the better lines that appear to be breeding on at the moment.

If it is possible try and acquire a bitch that has shown she can win a decent race and therefore has pace. Find a bitch that is dead honest, not one over whom there might be doubts, and not one, however well bred, who would not chase at all. You might be told, 'She was far too clever to chase the dummy; she knew it was not the real thing!' That is a load of rubbish. Honest Greyhounds will chase anything – the really good ones have the killer instinct to boot! It has also been said that it is a mistake to breed from bitches that have done a great deal of racing. I would agree with this as I feel it saps some of their stamina permanently; but there are exceptions, take Cranog Bet for example.

Let us look for a moment at the practice that is commonly called 'inbreeding'. Look at the extended pedigree of your bitch, which would go back five generations. The parents of your puppies are the first degree in relationship and the grandparents the second degree and so on. After the fourth degree I feel that little notice need be taken of the ancestors.

If the same dog's name appears more than once in the pedigree this is seen to be a consolidation of a certain blood strain. When a dog appears on the sire line and the dam line within the last four generations, this is called inbreeding. Line-breeding, on the other hand, is tracing the pedigree back on both sides to an outstanding dog and consolidating his bloodline. The most usual way to do this is to mate a dog with his dam's half-sister, so producing a preponderance of his maternal grandsire's blood.

It must be remembered that it is not the slightest use taking a paper pedigree and line-breeding on any dog or bitch without knowing anything about the dogs themselves and what you are hoping to achieve. The dominant traits are fairly easy to ascertain, such as pace and stamina, lack of injury proneness, and good sensible temperament. But, on the other hand, many of the recessive traits may not show themselves for a generation or two and those are the ones about which careful enquires have to be made. Bad mouths, monorchids or cryptorchids are faults that spring to mind, and, in fact, loss of vigour.

Line-breeding in Greyhounds is very difficult due to the fact that they do not show their true potential until they are at least two years old, by which time some of the ancestors that you might want have been lost, and you have then to try and find their best progeny with the traits that you are looking for.

More will be discussed on this subject when I give examples of today's bloodlines and some outstanding dogs and bitches.

Let's take a few costings now, the first being the stud fee. If you were to go to what is considered the most fashionable dog in Ireland at present it would set you back a cool £700. On top of that you have to take the bitch to Ireland yourself and give up at least two days to the task. The second most fashionable dog is, I believe, between £400 and £500 and I think that he is better bred. But of course not all stud fees are that huge.

However, when you are shelling out any large amount of money it is wise to try and make sure that everything with the bitch is right. Ask your vet to swab her. Some will do it before she comes in season and some hold the view that the bitch should have just started her season to get the best result. This practice is to make sure that there is no infection present in the uterus. If there is it is relatively simple for the vet to give a course of the correct antibiotic and clear up the problem before the mating day comes around.

When the bitch is safely mated you then have the expense of feeding her with the very best food and milk, plus supplements to ensure she has good healthy puppies. It will not do to feed her any old thing; a very high protein diet is indicated, and this costs money. So you may safely assume that for the next nine weeks your food bill will be in the region of £12 plus per week, which at a conservative estimate comes to over £100.

The great day arrives and with any luck your bitch will be delivered of a nice litter of eight puppies, mostly dogs. Any more than that for a first litter probably means running about with babies' bottles filled with Whelpie (extra expense) after the first week – I shall get to those problems later – but, hoping that there are not any more, your costs will rise for food and for electricity to service the heat lamp in the kennel. Small pups need a lot of heat. I would estimate that to get a litter to earmarking age, i.e. nine weeks old, it's going to cost all of another £150.

The registrations, inspection by the vet for same and the earmarking fees (which seem to go up every year to outstrip inflation), will set you back another £100 at least. So, all in all, it has cost you to get your litter to nine weeks old about £800 give or take a few hundred and that depends on the stud fee that you have to pay.

All these pessimistic paragraphs are designed to try and make you realise that before embarking on a breeding programme it is vital to get the best bitch you can for your venture and also to research the bloodlines.

Although the bitch that you are proposing to breed from is a crucial part in the programme it also follows that selecting the sire of your litter is very important as well. I should like to say here that too many people have their bitch come in season and then think that they would like to breed a litter. That's the wrong way to go about the job, bearing in mind the enormous costs of breeding and rearing. It would give you only fourteen days before the bitch is ready for the dog to work out all the breeding and choose the stud dog. That really is not long enough. Also, on a point that I have made before, your bitch should have a full booster inoculation before she is mated and it is wise to swab her too, so you would be rather busy in any case without the added work of choosing the right dog.

In many ways the choice of the stud dog can be governed by finance. This applies to us all, but it does not stop us being able to match the bloodlines and use a stud dog that is within our pockets. They are not all standing at fantastic fees and they would not be standing at all if they had nothing to recommend them. I think that it is a mistake though to use the most fashionable dog of the day with absolutely no regard to the bloodlines just because it would be a money-spinning exercise and the puppies would sell easily. I know that the majority of breeders have to sell some of the pups for the simple reason that most of them would not be able to afford to rear a whole litter of eight, shall

Puppies in the nest at a few days old.

we say. But having undertaken to breed a litter at all the important thing is to try to get everything right and breed a winner for yourself, in the hope that you might breed a Derby winner, an open race dog or, at any rate, a decent pup that you will be able to have a lot of enjoyment with. In the section on bloodlines we shall be trying to give a guide on what lines are breeding on and which lines seem to hit together. They do change from year to year as new dogs come on the scene, but with a little background information it's not too hard to study the pedigrees of the current or recent winning dogs.

The gestation period of the bitch is nine weeks, or sixty-three days, but they don't always whelp on the right day. If there are not many puppies they are quite often a day or so late. Anything up to about four days is acceptable but after that time it would be wise to consult your vet in case there are dead puppies or some other problem. If the bitch is very heavy the puppies may arrive a day or two early, but that is not really anything to worry about.

The whelping kennel and bed should be made ready well in advance. The arrangements for the heat lamp should be fixed properly so that there is not a mad and disturbing rush at the last minute. The bitch should be introduced to her kennel when all is ready, at least ten to fourteen days prior to whelping. Pregnant bitches need to get properly settled and accept that this is their place, then they should have their puppies without too much stress and be quite happy. It is a good idea to site the kennel in a quiet corner so that there is not too much coming and going around them.

The illustrated whelping unit is a self-contained arrangement which can be readily housed in any suitable building that has an electricity supply. The whole structure is on wheels and the slatted floor is raised 6 ins (150 mm) so that all the wet drops on to the sawdust below. This then can easily be cleaned by simply moving the unit.

The slatted floor prevents the bedding becoming saturated but it does rather depend on what bedding you use. Wood wool seems to work very well with this unit; paper tends to go soggy. Paper should not be used until the pups are really very strong and waddling about as it's rather dangerous for very young ones. Not only do they get underneath it and can then get squashed by the bitch who may not see them, but also they get the strands of paper wrapped around themselves and can be strangled. 'Drybed' is very good. The wet goes through leaving the top dry and it is washable.

The best thing to actually whelp the bitch on is ordinary newspaper. It can be changed very easily and burnt, and when the bitch is whelping

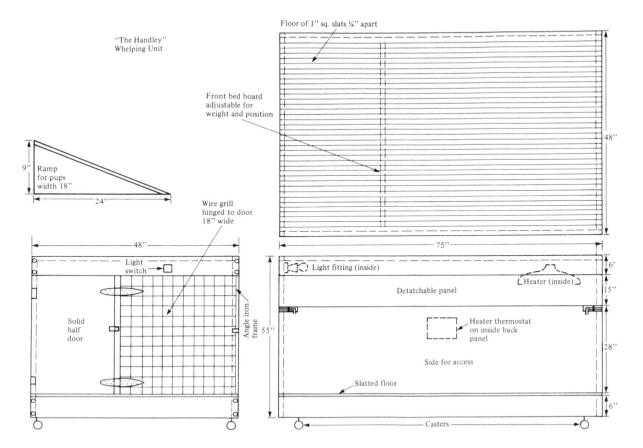

"The Handley"
Whelping Unit

Floor of 1" sq. slats ¼" apart

Front bed board
adjustable for
weight and position

9" Ramp
for pups
width 18"

24"

Wire grill
hinged to door
18" wide

48"

Light
switch

Solid
half
door

Angle iron
frame

55"

48"

75"

Light fitting (inside)

Heater (inside)

Detatchable panel

Heater thermostat
on inside back
panel

Side for access

Slatted floor

Casters

6'

15"

28"

6"

she tends to tear everything up, so newspaper can economically be replaced. Usually I leave the newspaper on the bed for three or four days while the bitch is cleansing, and then I change to either Dry Bed or squares of carpet to fit the whelping box. These can be changed every two days or so, scrubbed and replaced when dry. Carpet is nice and warm and also gives the pups something to grip on; with a smooth surface their hind legs slip away from under them when they are sucking and it must be very tiring for them.

I have a large box, 4 ft × 4 ft (120 cm²) with 9 in. (225 mm) sides, with a piece cut out in the front and hinged and bolted, so that when the pups start trying to climb out it can be opened to make a door for them. There are some whelping boxes advertised which stand on legs, but unless you have very high sides the pups can fall out and hurt themselves. A ramp could be attached to these but it would have to be quite wide and with cross bars fastened onto it for the pups to grip on.

When the time comes for the birth most bitches get pretty restless.

FIG. 7 Whelping unit.

They rip up the bed and lie there puffing and panting; this is quite natural. They will sometimes pant for a whole day before they settle down to some serious straining. I once had a Dalmatian bitch who, instead of bothering to pant, used to shriek and howl for hours. The neighbourhood must have thought I was killing her. Once that stage was over she never made a sound.

The serious straining will carry on anything from twenty minutes to two hours. Any longer and it may mean you have to seek help, but first take the bitch for a walk. The walking quite often moves the first pup on a bit and the bitch may urinate, which relieves the pressure on the bladder. I remember one bitch who refused to have her pups unless we took her out for a walk, then she would squat down and drop them on the lawn. You can imagine what it was like in the dead of winter – one person leading the bitch and me running round behind with a torch and a large towel to wrap the newborn pup in. This would go on all night, the same procedure for each pup. It was quite a performance.

I wouldn't think it wise to allow serious straining to go on for more than three hours without calling the vet, but you would be quite unlucky if this happened. It's usually due to a breech, a very big pup arriving first, or a dead pup. This is one of the reasons why it is easier to breed from a good-sized bitch; this kind of problem is more likely to occur with a very small bitch.

However, once you have the first pup and the bitch has cleaned it, the afterbirth comes away and she is ready for the next one to appear. If the bitch is very clumsy I tend to have a hot-water bottle ready in a box, covered with a blanket, and I put the pups in there to keep warm while she has the others. Mostly, though, they are pretty careful and manage to avoid squashing them; and after the first there is not much bother with the rest. Large litters seem to arrive with great speed and very small litters take ages in between pups.

When you think your bitch has finished and seems settled with her litter, it is wise to ask your vet to come and have a look just to make sure that she has cleared everything. More than likely he will give her an injection to help contract the uterus and thereby expel any afterbirth that might be left inside.

Once she is comfortable with her litter and has had a nice drink of warm milk with a beaten egg in it, plus a good tablespoon of glucose, you can leave her to sleep for an hour or two. It is sensible to try and get her up fairly soon so that she goes and empties herself. Many bitches will burst before they leave the pups during the first day or two, but a little gentle persuasion usually works. While she is out you can change the newspaper and clear up all the rubbish. As stated I leave my bitches on newspaper for about three days, by which time the worst of the discharge is over.

For the next ten days or so until the pups' eyes open, all you need do is feed the bitch well and make sure that the pups are all sucking. A contented litter will make little snuffling noises and moans; if the pups are making a querulous noise and sound discontented make sure that the bitch has enough milk. At this stage if you squeeze the teats you should always get milk; if not, the vet will give something to try and stimulate the flow. Some bitches can, for various reasons, be short of milk, but not many, thank heaven.

If this does happen to your bitch try and keep the pups on her but two or three times a day feed the pups yourself on Whelpie from a bottle. Modern baby bottles work very well and I have suggested Whelpie (details of which will be found in Appendix A) because I have had quite a lot of success with it. There are other compounds, however, and here again the vet would know all about the most up-to-date one and advise you. Whatever you use in your bottle, be sure to adhere rigidly to the manufacturer's instructions. The compound will have been extensively tested and deviating from the recommended guide-lines can give problems, the most usual one being scouring.

Puppies soon get used to sucking a bottle and this will tide you over until after their eyes open and you can begin the feeding routine. The diet sheet for this is given in Appendix A.

Pups should be handled from a very early age, but not by all and sundry. Do it yourself. They like a cuddle even before their eyes are properly open and it does wonders for their outlook on life later on.

Another reason for a discontented sound from your litter might be that they are cold. It is very important to realise that during the first few days they need what you might feel to be a very hot environment. I have a heat lamp set in such a way that it does not cause distress to the bitch, about 3 ft (1 m) from the bottom of the bed, and make sure that it is fastened securely to the roof. After two or three days, assuming that the weather is quite warm, you can raise it and later on turn it off during the day. Either red or white bulbs are available for these lamps, and I always use the white ones. I do this not because the amount of heat from them is any better but because it means you can see more clearly and that is important during the first few days.

If the dew claws are to be removed from the pups, have it done at about three to four days. If they happen to have them on the back legs they must be removed in any case, but I also think that the front ones should be taken off. Later on in life, dew claws, particularly prominent ones, are inclined to get broken and if they have to be removed at that stage it involves a major operation. There is no point, to my mind, in keeping them – I can't see what use they are.

The management of a litter during the first four weeks of life hinges mainly on two things. The first is cleanliness, and the second feeding. It is very important to keep the bed dry and clean and to do that your bedding, whatever you use, needs changing every two to three days. As I have said before, I use squares of carpet to fit the whelping box. I have three pieces cut to size so that there is one in the bed, one spare, and one in the wash. It's quite easy to scrub the soiled piece with a solution of Dettol, but drying it is not always so easy in the winter. A radiator comes in useful for this. It's not wise to use very thick carpet as it's unmanageable. The foam-backed type is quite adequate and fairly easy to wash. The Dry Bed that is obtainable from pet shops is also very good and easier to manage than carpet, but being thin it tends to ruck up all the time.

As soon as the pups are toddling about open the little gate in the box and let them walk out. Cover the outside floor with good quality sawdust and you will be quite surprised how soon they go away from the bed to empty and tiddle. They should be encouraged as soon as they are well on their feet to go outside – not only does the fresh air do them good but also it teaches them to be clean at a very early age. The only thing that must be watched is the arrangement at the door so that (a) the door can't slam on them and (b) they are able to negotiate the step easily. With these two points taken care of they can go in and out at will and if it rains there are not many who will sit out in it and get soaked.

I never shut the pups' shed door, even at night, unless the weather is very bad, and I would say that from eight weeks on this practice is quite safe. As long as they have a dry bed and a warm corner to go to they won't come to much harm.

The diet sheets for puppies in Appendix A also give help on the type of dishes that are easy to manage and on how to start feeding the pups. The diet sheets are pretty well self-explanatory and can be kept to with complete confidence. After twelve weeks the further diet sheets give the choice of what method of feeding suits you best.

Take your vet's advice about when to give the Parvo inoculations. It seems a good idea to give just a Parvo injection at about six weeks and then do the whole lot in the proper sequence starting at twelve weeks.

Another thing that you would be well advised to do is take your vet's advice on a worming regime. I start worming my pups not later than four weeks old. To start with I use a liquid wormer that I get from the vet. The pups need doing about every three weeks until they are fourteen weeks old. As a general rule the only worms that you will get are roundworms but they need keeping in check. It helps if you worm your brood bitch before she is mated.

At ten weeks, when you have finished all the form filling and other red tape that is required, the pups should be earmarked. They have to be kept together as a litter until this is done and your nearest earmarking steward will come and do this for you. The Greyhound Stud Book will arrange with the NGRC for this to be done and normally the steward will get in touch to arrange a suitable day. I am afraid that most pups get a bit upset over this but in about a week they will have forgotten it all and should be back to normal.

Once all these things have been done, and that includes the inoculations, you will be ready to sell those pups you wish to dispose of and make rearing arrangements for the remainder. Later on it is quite the norm to get bullying within a litter, so if you are splitting the group, try and put friends together. It is quite easy to see which ones play and are happy together and which one gets the worst of the bullying. So divide your litter accordingly.

Another point that needs some discussion is the question of 'fading puppies'. This problem is not quite so prevalent as it used to be, mainly due to the swabbing of bitches and the increased standards of hygiene. However, it can still happen and the signs are that in ones and twos the pups during their first week begin to get very weak and finally die. Very often the bitch will tell you which are the fading ones: she will push them away into a corner. She knows what will live and what won't and perhaps we should pay more attention to her. My litters have not suffered from this syndrome for many years but an Irish company, Duphar Ireland Ltd, has developed a vaccine called Duphapind. They claim that this is a great help if you have the problem or feel that you are likely to get it. The details of their product will be found in Appendix C. In any event it would be prudent to contact your vet immediately you have any suspicions about the litter.

Eclampsia is the other problem that you might come across. This happens about two hours after whelping and is, in effect, the same as milk-fever in cattle. The level of calcium in the bitch drops dramatically. You will see extreme distress and the bitch will stagger round the kennel before collapsing. 'Stagger' is the operative word, and the moment that you see anything like this you must get the vet with all speed because the bitch has to have a large dose of calcium by injection at once. Once administered, the effects are quite miraculous – the bitch recovers in a matter of minutes and is perfectly normal again. However, speed is of the essence and unless action is taken at once the bitch will go into a coma and die. I have had just one case of this. Perhaps one way of preventing it is to give proper doses of calcium before whelping. I think that very excitable bitches may be more prone to this problem. However, don't worry too much – it is relatively rare.

Handling and Management of Stud Dogs

Normally when a dog is retired to stud he will have been in a racing kennel up until that time and when he arrives if he has been used to being kennelled with a bitch this should be continued. The routine that he has been used to should not be altered to any great extent, mainly because if he is simply left on the bed, as it were, he will get bored and feel he has been abandoned.

The feeding should be the same as for racing dogs and his weight should be kept to not more than a pound or two over his racing weight. There is nothing worse than to see stud dogs being allowed to get fat and flabby, and, indeed, quite unfit for anything.

Particular attention should be paid to his teeth and nails. As they get older the teeth tend to deteriorate – this happens with all dogs. I realise that if you are running a busy kennel it is not always possible to brush the dogs' teeth every day, but a marrow-bone every now and then is a good idea. This should be offered in an empty kennel so that it is not all covered with sawdust and paper bedding! Also, never give a bone where there are two dogs together as that always leads to a fight.

Nails are also very important. They require cutting regularly and keeping as short as possible. When the dog begins his stud duties if his nails are long he will inflict a good deal of discomfort on the visiting bitches when he mounts them.

It is not a good idea to kennel your stud dog with another dog. It leads to jealousy and he does not want to spend the rest of his life with a muzzle on his head. So, if you haven't a bitch to put him with he should have a good kennel on his own where he can watch what goes on, see people and in fact is not shut away. Stud dogs need to be treated the same as an open race dog to get the best results from them.

When introducing the stud dog to his first bitch, ideally you need a bitch that has been mated before, not a maiden bitch. They are more sensible and less likely to get upset and in turn upset the dog. One has to realise when starting a dog on his stud career that during his racing days he will have been strongly discouraged from bothering about bitches at all, and therefore may assume to start with that he is doing something wrong.

The key word at this stage is 'patience' and plenty of it. If the weather is reasonable it is a nice idea to embark on his first venture outside on the grass. You must choose a really quiet spot that is not used by other dogs, so that there are not too many alluring smells to take his mind from the job in hand, and one where he cannot be distracted by other dogs rushing around barking and so forth. Many young stud dogs take to the job like ducks to water but some don't and anyway too many distractions are a bad thing.

If he is a shy dog it is not a good idea for the first time to have the owner of the bitch with you to start with. Once he gets into the routine it is a good thing for the owner to be there to stand in front of the bitch holding her. Apart from the owner, you need one assistant and the person who is actually handling the dog. Your assistant squats down on the left-hand side of the bitch and holds her underneath the brisket to stop her moving around too much. The person handling the dog stands behind letting the dog know he or she is there so that the dog gets used to that routine. By letting the dog do the job on his own in the first instance they tend to get awkward to handle.

It is usually necessary to lubricate the bitch, and the best thing to use is KY Jelly, which can be obtained from any chemist. It is not very hygienic to use Vaseline; I don't like to see people sticking their fingers in a pot of this because, for one thing, you can easily transfer infection by this method. KY Jelly can be squeezed from the tube directly onto the bitch. With a maiden bitch it may be necessary to explore inside to ascertain whether she is very tight and to do this disposable sterilised gloves can be used, which again reduce the risk of infection to the bitch.

If the bitch is very tight inside it does tend to put off a young stud dog. This can be a problem with a first bitch for your dog. Once they are used to their job it makes no difference.

When the dog has mounted, the handler can hold the bitch by her stifles and guide the dog into the bitch. In the first instance, when he has his first bitch, he probably will jump off and on a few times.

As soon as the dog starts striking at the bitch it's a good idea to let him know that you are there, and, having guided him in, put your hand under his bottom and push. By that time the assistant who is squatting will have risen to support the dog so that he does not fall over left or right, and stays up for two or three minutes so that he effects a firm tie. The proper and natural method is to turn the dog, and the dog is less inclined to hurt himself in any way if this is done.

What you do is this. While the handler is still holding the dog tight onto the bitch at the back, the assistant puts his left hand under the dog's neck and brings his right hand over to take hold of the dog's off fore. As he brings the dog over he is still supporting the dog with his left hand. He then uses his right hand to bring the back right leg over also. This way your dog is painlessly turned, and dog and the bitch are standing back to back. From then on the handler holds them close together and they can be like this for anything from ten minutes up to half an hour.

Using this method there is no reason why the dogs should hurt themselves. It is, however, very important with a young dog having his first bitch that he is not allowed to get into too much of a stew and get tired. If you find that he is not going to mate the bitch very easily, the best thing is to put him back in his kennel, keep him well away from the bitch and go and have a cup of tea. You can then try again later and hope to win. If, in fact, you can't effect the mating the best thing to do is to ask the owner to leave the bitch or else bring her back the next day.

If you are really in trouble and feel that you are not going to get a particular bitch mated I think it is only fair that you should tell the owner. This then gives him the chance to make arrangements to use another dog rather than miss the bitch for another six or nine months. It's fairly rare to encounter insurmountable problems, and it's largely a matter of getting to know your dog.

In the event the dog is very lively and works himself into a great sweat over the job, and, provided he is sound, it's a good idea to give him a couple of hundred yards gallop' in the early morning of the mating day. Stud dogs need the normal amount of exercise in any case; if they are crippled you can put them out in a large paddock to potter round at will. They should be treated like any other dog in the kennel because, after all, they are a valuable commodity.

Once the dog is mating his bitches nicely outside it's a good idea to take him inside, again finding a quiet, secluded room. It's no use putting the pair on a shiny surface; a large square of thick carpet is ideal for them to stand on. It is important when you are starting a young dog on his stud career to go always to the same spot outside and the same place inside so that the connection is made that this is the place for him to do his job.

Having got through the first mating all right, it makes sense for him to have another bitch quite quickly. Ideally, he could serve three bitches in about ten days. After that it is in the lap of the gods. In England it is unusual for stud dogs to be over-used.

If for some reason the dog was required to mate the same bitch twice it could be done the next day provided the dog was in good order, otherwise leaving a day in between. Never leave it longer than one day.

Some dogs find the whole business slightly difficult and one of the problems can be that they seem to be embarrassed about the job. If so, it is a good idea to have with you only people whom the dog knows. The owner of the bitch should stay away until you have the dogs safely tied and then he can come and see that his bitch has had a successful mating.

I think we should now mention the really difficult dogs. Some will mount a bitch and then just hang there or fall off without attempting to do anything. In cases like this you have to resort to manipulation. Get your hand as far back between his legs as possible, and rub gently. This will usually result in encouraging him to strike at the bitch. But at all times the dog must be used to being handled. It is absolutely no use turning him into a paddock or loose box and letting him get on with it. This merely results for the most part in him making a hash of the job and getting thoroughly exhausted. It's very difficult to tell anybody exactly how to manipulate the dog, but if you do what I have said the idea will most likely fall into place. Sometimes you will get a strong reaction, at others a weak one; but if you are able to guide the dog into the bitch they usually get the idea and if you then push hard you should effect a tie.

In some cases you have to actually lift the dog onto the bitch because he won't mount her on his own. This might be due to having been strongly discouraged from bothering with bitches in the early years. The dog simply feels he is doing wrong.

When he has effected his first mating, be sure to give the dog plenty of praise and make a fuss of him, telling him what a good boy he is. This encourages him to do even better next time.

There are a few general rules to observe for matings. Always make sure that both dog and bitch are thoroughly emptied before you start. It is not a good idea to start a mating when the participants have a full bladder. Always muzzle the bitch and have another muzzle handy so that, if required, you can muzzle the dog. Some dogs have been known to get very bad-tempered just before they are released from the bitch at the end of the tie. They won't bite the bitch but they might bite the handler. It is best to use the Beaverwood type of muzzle with plenty of air space in it. The muzzle can be removed from the bitch once she is safely tied, because she may tend to get hot and puffed. It is to be hoped that bitches arrive when they are really right and this seems to make it much easier for the dog. At the end of the day the whole operation boils down to patience and kindness, so that you build up confidence in your dog and he trusts you to handle and help him with his job.

There is a series of pictures showing exactly how to mate a bitch from start to finish, and I hope that these will be helpful until the handler of the stud dog gets the hang of the job.

This sequence of photographs illustrates the correct way to mate a bitch.

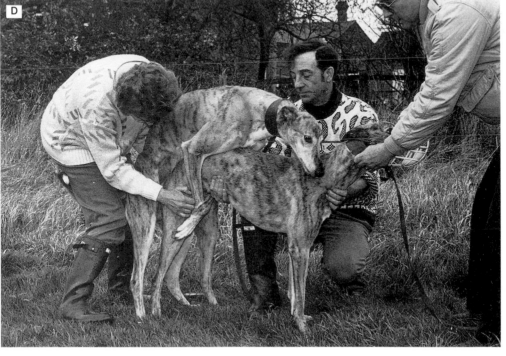

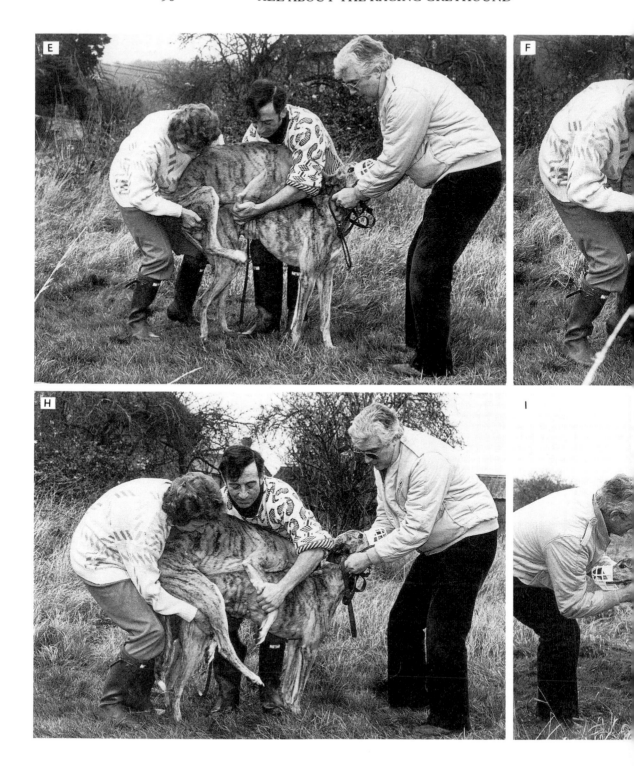

7 Stud Dogs and Bloodlines

There is never any shortage of Greyhounds standing at stud in England and Ireland. The selection of the sire when breeding a litter should be given careful consideration.

You should take into account the pedigree and performance of the dog and whether he excelled on the track or in the coursing field. Generally speaking, there are three distinctly different types and today's breeder would be well advised to recognise this fact.

Whereas sixty years ago all track Greyhounds came from coursing stock, today the division is very marked indeed. A careful study of the pedigrees of the champions of the track shows hardly any coursing bloodlines closer than the fourth or fifth generation. Similarly the finalists at Clonmel (park coursing) have no recognised track lines. These coursing dogs are bred to be big and fast, and can weigh up to 100 lbs (45 kg). In my view they are not Waterloo Cup types at all.

The English coursing dog at stud may have a line of track blood, possibly going back to Hi There, but he will have to have been stout-hearted and a good worker to command any respect from the coursing breeder.

There are a few stud dogs that stand out as having a great influence on the breeding pattern of the track dogs. Hi There was a fantastic sire of track dogs and greatly influenced the breeding pattern of the fifties and sixties. His sons, all great dogs themselves, i.e. Crazy Parachute, Prairie Flash, Tontine, Printers Prince, Low Pressure, Crazy Society, completely dominated the next ten years as sires of good track Greyhounds. The most successful and most widely used son of Crazy Parachute ex Sheila at Last was Monalee Champion who then dominated the next period by producing a wealth of good dogs and bitches.

His sons have produced and still are producing some very dominant stock. For example, Sole Aim (sire of Knockrour Slave); Jimsun (sire of Sarah's Bunny); Monalee Hiker (sire of Glenroe Hiker); It's a Champion (sire of Lacca Champion); Linda's Champion (grandsire of

Tico through the dam line, i.e. Derry Linda) also produced in that same litter Jaguar and O'Hickey Garden. Jaguar was a very good dog in Ireland and O'Hickey Garden was injured early but showed great promise. In the litter to Game Ball, Derry Linda produced Droopy's Jaguar who won the Clonmel Produce Stakes in 1987. Ballinderry Moth, the dam of Derry Linda, is from that now-famous Skipping Tim–Mayfield Chick line and on the sire's side goes back to the great dam Clonmoney Grand, who was the mother of Kilbelin Style. As a matter of interest, Daley's Gold was Derry Linda's full brother from a later litter. He was a great sprinter and won the Scurry Cup in 1985.

It is also interesting to note that Lackandarra, dam of 1987 Scurry Cup finalist Up for One, is an older full sister to Daleys Gold. She is from the litter which included Swift Rapier, Desert Moth Westpark Goldie (dam of Hot Sauce Yankee), Westpark Moth (won Shelbourne Leger) and Derry Linda (dam of Tico). It is generally agreed that the introduction of some American blood, by way of Bright Lad, Peco's Jerry and later by Sandman and Sail On 11, came at the right moment because at the time Greyhound breeding had become saturated with Hi There blood. It did not appear that the outcross to the coursing lines was very successful for the track, possibly with the exception of Jack Mullans' dam line going right back to Millie's May, who in turn produced the bitch Racing Millie to Man of Pleasure. Racing Millie was the dam of Lucky Wonder and Wonder Valley when mated to Pigalle Wonder. April Merry was the litter sister of those two dogs.

Bright Lad and Peco's Jerry (sire of the only triple Scurry winner Yankee Express) threw early-paced animals, while Sandman, when crossed with Irish/English bitches, absolutely took off with early paced, middle-distance runners and stayers of Classic qualities. Sandman's great sons include Game Ball, Express Opinion, Dipmac and Whisper Wishes. It is interesting to note that Bright Lad, when mated to the bitch Letesia, produced Minnesota Miller and, from a later litter, Minnesota Mark, both of whom won the Waterloo Cup.

There are no hard and fast rules regarding breeding the type of Greyhound that you require. Many sprint dogs throw great stayers, but without statistics to prove it our feeling is that this comes from the dam lines on both sides. As an example the Westmeads always produce dogs that run on strongly no matter what sire they use with their dam lines. Also, we feel that it might be that trainers of sprinters will not try them over a longer trip for fear of taking the edge from their early pace.

As a short cut, a breeder can only go to a proven sire who is continually producing trackers of a certain type.

Newdown Heather, who was very extensively used at stud, did not appear to produce many exceptional stud dogs, with the exception of Supreme Fun, but he seemed to produce bitches that in their turn made very good broods. Supreme Fun sired Laurdella Fun and Waverly Supreme. The latter was exported to Australia and was by far the most successful sire out there of his time.

Laurdella Fun, when mated to Flying Lady (from the Skipping Chick, Kilbelin Style line), produced Brilliant Chimes, who is having a great impact on the breeding scene today. His litter brother, Ballyderg Fox, stands at stud in England. I'm Slippy, from the mating of Laurdella Fun to Glenroe Bess, is definitely breeding on. So far, to a selection of bitches, he has produced Murlen's Slippy, Monroe Luck, Copper King, Slip the Lot, Lavally Oak and the amazing young dog Aulton Slippy, whose mother is Oran Beauty by Minnesota Miller Spooky Lady. Spooky Lady is the mother of Oran Jack. Also in I'm Slippy's litter was Glenroe Blue, who is making a limited impact at stud. Their mother, Glenroe Bess, to Dipmac produced Metro Express, who would have done well in the 1987 Derby had he not damaged a tendon.

We have spoken about Tico's mother but not yet about The Stranger, his sire. Interestingly enough he is also the sire of Tapwatcher, who was most unlucky not to win the 1987 Derby. Both Derry Linda and her sister O'Hickey Silver were mated to The Stranger in 1986. They might produce another Tico.

Of the English broods Sarah's Bunny has produced open race dogs in every litter. To Desert Pilot, there were Golden Sand and Disco Stardust. To Ron Hardy, there were Fearless Action, Fearless Swift and Master Hardy. To Mountkeefe Star, there were Fearless Ace and Fearless Flight who were first and second in the Bristol Produce Stakes. To Special Account, there was Fearless Champ.

The other main line in English breeding is, of course, the Westmeads. The two brood bitches, Hacksaw, by Hack up Chieftain, and Cricket Dance, by Prairie Flash, have been prolific producers of open race dogs and bitches: Westmead County by Clonalvy Pride–Cricket Dance; Westmead Champ by Westmead County–Hacksaw; Westmead Power by Westmead County–Westmead Damson; Westmead Milos by All Wit–Westmead Satin, who was by Westmead Lane–Hacksaw. Westmead Move, who after a great career has now been retired for breeding, is by Whisper Wishes–Westmead Tania (Glenroe Hiker–Westmead Satin). In this litter there were also Westmead Call and Oliver's Wish.

Jane Hicks, of Holm Farm near Horsham, established herself as a breeder of considerable merit in the six years from 1980–86. Her foundation bitch King's Comet, by Cobbler ex Robin Silver, had already had two litters to Myrtown and after Jane Hicks acquired her her son Sir Winston won the Grand National. Mated to Peco's Jerry she produced Copper Beeches and Yankee Express. The latter turned out to be the first of George Curtis's record-breakers, being the first dog in England to win a Classic on the flat three times, i.e. the Scurry Cup.

Breeze Valley, a daughter of Glin Bridge, when she retired whelped her first litter to Knockrour Brandy and from that litter, among other names, came The Jolly Norman Derby finalist in 1984. The 1984 litter Yankee Express–Breeze Valley produced She Wolf, the winner of the Breeders' Forum Produce Stakes. Lone Wolf from the same litter won the 1986 Leger.

King's Lace (Myrtown–King's Comet) visited Cosmic Sailor and from that union came Yankee Shadow. She won the Regency at Brighton, the Key at Wimbledon, the Cesarewitch at Belle Vue and for good measure broke the 880-metres track record at Walthamstow, which in 1987 she still holds.

In 1968 Richard Handley started the Breeders' Forum. David Poulter was the Chairman and Richard Handley the Secretary. It was envisaged that an organisation such as this would help to improve British breeding. The Breeders' Festival was first held at The Hook Kennels, Northaw, but in 1975 it moved to Harringay, and in 1984 to Picketts Lock, where it is now held. It is a very good thing and gives those interested in breeding a chance to see good brood bitches and some of the dogs that are standing at stud in this country.

Unfortunately, apart from Mr and Mrs Savva, Geoffrey de Mulder, Jane Hicks and Mr Fenwick of the 'Gan On' prefix from Northumberland, the incidents of breeding in this country appear to be more or less one-off litters. There are plenty of litters and the numbers have increased dramatically in recent years, mainly due I would think to the influence and help given to would-be breeders by the Forum, with the incentives of the Produce Stakes and the British Breeders' race, which I was lucky enough to win one year with Tilbrook Herald. Possibly the one-off cases are due to the difficulty in rearing pups and finding enough free range for them to grow in, making a continuous programme impossible for many would-be breeders.

The mainstay of the 'Gan On' dogs was the bitch Midi Robin by Wonderful Era out of Lovely Robin. Mr McAllister is currently

Three of the great personalities in Greyhound racing photographed in 1970 at Northaw Festival. At the back is J. Edwards Clarke, author of many books on the Greyhound, on the left is Jimmy Jowett and on the right is Richard Handley, founder of the Greyhound Breeders' Forum.

breeding from two of her daughters by Linacre–Midi Robin and seems very pleased with the results. Mr Fenwick has Honeymoon Trish, a daughter of Honeymoon Band, who was the litter sister of Linacre and the only bitch in that litter. She has been mated to Rail Fred, a very prolific winner in this country whose mother, Crooked Rampart, was the litter sister of Peruvian Style. She was also the mother of Blacker's Height from her litter to Bright Lad.

The world record holder, Ballyregan Bob.

The breeding scene would not be quite complete without mentioning the record-breakers. Westpark Mustard and Peruvian Style both broke Mick the Miller's record of nineteen consecutive wins. However, since then we have had the great Ballyregan Bob who smashed the lot and got himself a new world record with thirty-two consecutive wins. He is an outstanding dog, but then he also had an outstanding trainer. He was by Ballyheigue Moon–Evening Daisy. In the same litter was Evening Light, also a prolific open race winner.

In Ireland the main breeders seem to go on from year to year and become associated with the dogs that they have bred. Leslie McNair founded his strain on the Knockhill dogs. He bought Cranog Bet and she produced many open race winners for him, It's a Champion probably being the most famous. The late Jack Mullans bred Lucky Wonder and Wonder Valley from his bitch Racing Millie, and many others including Kerry Wonder from the bitch Swanky Echo.

The late Jack McAllister bred the Crazy dogs; Paddy Dunphy bred and owned The Grand Canal, The Grand Champion and The Grand Fire ... I could go on for ever. Possibly the reason why they continue from year to year is that it is in their blood and they have much more space than we do for rearing. It should also be realised that breeding Greyhounds is one of the main industries in Ireland. It is unfortunate that in recent years the price of Irish Greyhounds has gone 'beyond the pale' and I feel that many people have reached the stage where they will not pay these 'telephone numbers' for young dogs that have only won one race in a decent time, quite possibly in a box full of mediocre dogs. One feels that perhaps this trend has got out of hand and it will eventually 'kill the goose that lays the golden eggs'.

There is just one interesting point that breeders should consider and that is the question of colour inheritance. Coat colour is the result of a combination of four factors:

Background. This will either be black or brown, the black being the dominant colour.

Pattern. This is either black or brown striping and, again, the black striping is dominant.

Whiteness. This can either be normal, white chest, toes and tail end, or parti-coloured, half the coat being white. Normal is dominant.

Dilution. This alters the colour of a black coat to blue and a fawn coat to blue-brindle or blue-fawn. Normal colour is dominant over dilute.

These four factors (without making it too complicated) give rise to certain rules of thumb:
(1) White/fawn mated to white/fawn can only produce white/fawn offspring.
(2) Black pups can only be produced if one or both parents are black, white/black or blue, which is dilute black.
(3) Stud dogs who are black or white/black always produce black or white/black pups in a litter, no matter to what bitch they are mated. Newdown Heather was a classic example of this last rule. His colour

was very dominant and I believe that he only produced black or white and black pups.

On the back of the stud forms issued in Ireland there is a note about colour inheritance, and if, for instance, black or white and black puppies turn up in a litter where there should be none, the stud book is questioning breeders where this arises. There are several books written by experts on genetics in the dog and anyone interested should study them.

8 The Racing Scene

In 1926 an American, C. A. Munn, Major Lyne Dixon and Brigadier General A. C. Critchley staged the first proper Greyhound meeting at Belle Vue, Manchester, with races for seven dogs.

In 1927 Celtic Park opened its doors and Greyhound racing started in Ireland. This was closely followed by the opening of Shelbourne Park.

The White City in London opened in June 1927, closely followed by Harringay in September 1927 both under the GRA banner and Clapton in April 1928. Wembley Stadium opened for Greyhound Racing in December 1927.

Sadly, in recent years, due to the escalation of land values, many of the GRA tracks have closed to make room for yet more concrete jungles. Many other companies with Greyhound tracks have unfortunately gone the same way and there are all too few of the original tracks left now after sixty years.

The first official body to be formed in this country was the National Coursing Club in 1858, and the first Stud Book appeared in 1882 with 419 entries. In 1883 the compulsory registration of dogs was started. Until 1916 the National Coursing Club dealt with registrations and controlled coursing in Ireland as well as England. In this year the Irish Greyhound Stud Book was formed.

The National Greyhound Racing Society was formed in 1927 and fifty years later in 1977 became the British Greyhound Racing Federation. This has since folded and in its place we have the British Greyhound Racing Board, which was set up in 1979.

The BGRB consists of two sections: the Board of Directors and the Consultative Body, both of which are chaired by Lord Newall. The Board of Directors consists of the Chairman and Deputy Chairman, the Senior Steward of the NGRC, two representatives of the promoters, one each of greyhound breeders, professional trainers and greyhound owners. The Consultative Body consists of the eight

(OPPOSITE)
Patsy Byrne's Stouke Whisper after winning the Select Stakes in 1987.

Directors of the Board plus two additional representatives of the promoters, another breeder, trainer and owner, plus a veterinary surgeon and a greyhound on-course bookmaker.

In 1928 the National Greyhound Racing Club was started to organise Greyhound racing and formulate the rules of racing, register the tracks, the Greyhounds, trainers and staff.

In recent years the advent of betting shops, bingo halls, colour television, and various other leisure pursuits, has been instrumental in luring the public away from the tracks, and because of this managements and trainers alike have been having a very hard time.

Since the advent of betting shops in 1961 the attendance figures at the Greyhound tracks have fallen from fifteen million to four million and forty-four NGRC tracks have closed. This is not entirely due to the betting shops but, as I have pointed out, to the escalating value of the sites upon which the tracks stood and, last but not least, the purchase of some of the tracks by the big bookmakers. Ladbrokes originally owned seven tracks but have closed five of them but replaced Crayford Stadium with a new smaller track. Corals, a subsidiary of the Bass Group, have improved the two tracks that they own and have spent a great deal of money on both the tracks themselves and the facilities for the public. It seems that those tracks are there to stay.

However, it must be said that the NGRC and in particular its Secretary, Fred Underhill OBE, have been untiring in their efforts to get the government to appreciate the problem. They have now relaxed the race-days law and made it possible for the tracks to race on as many days as they wish, apart from Sundays and Good Friday of course.

Also, the government has seen fit to remove the on-course betting tax of 4%. This applies to the Tote and the bookmakers alike. The official figures for attendances and Tote turnover for the first six months of 1987 show a substantial increase: a rise of 7.4% in attendance and 16.7% in Tote turnover. This is a great boost for Greyhound racing and is entirely due, I believe, to the Government relaxing the race-days rule and removing the on-course betting duty.

I understand that the government, in spite of the enormous amount of work done by the NGRC to put before the Royal Commission the case for a levy similar to the one that horse racing enjoys, still refuses to accept their plea. One of the reasons is, I understand, that the Totes belong to the track managements and are not run by a central board, in the way horse racing Tote is.

It does, however, seem to me that the bookmakers who deduct a percentage from their clients' winnings to feed the Horse Racing Levy Board, also deduct the same percentage from the Greyhound bets that they handle. This money simply goes into their already bulging pockets and when asked what they do with it various feeble reasons emerge, one of which is to pay their expenses such as light, heating, rent and rates. This surely is nothing short of downright dishonesty.

It seems that the government should step in and grant Greyhound racing a levy which it badly needs and this would make it independent of the big bookmaking firms who control the majority of the betting shops. They also control between them the tracks that supply the BAGS service, or at any rate four of them, which puts any negotiations for more payment for the service in an invidious position. At present there is a storm blowing up between the BGRB and BAGS regarding the payment for the afternoon meetings that are staged for the benefit of the betting shops. The NGRC and the BGRB feel, quite rightly, that they should have the same stake in the new SIS (Satellite Information Service) company as has been granted to horse racing via the Racecourse Association, but it appears that SIS, who are controlled by the bookmakers and the Tote, are not prepared to talk.

All this is politics at the moment, but the outcome will one day be history.

The Permit Tracks, which started in 1974–75, went quite a long way to helping the enthusiastic Greyhound owner. They made it possible for owners to have a licence to train their own Greyhounds or those of their immediate family. Like every other concession in this world and where rules are relaxed, it has led to some abuses by a small minority of sharks who are only in the sport for the fun of pulling strokes and unfortunately it continues to give the overall scene a bad name. Whilst in some cases I find it hard to follow the reasoning of the NGRC in connection with some of the rules, I accept that the sport must have a ruling body. The NGRC rules do give some protection to the general public and this is of the utmost importance.

There has been some talk of the bookmaker-owned tracks going it alone, without the benefit of the licence from the NGRC for their racing operation, but when it comes to the crunch they really need the credibility that the NGRC rules and standards provide.

The recent report by the Monopolies Commission made some interesting comments, but it seems that the non-NGRC track managements are dragging their feet somewhat in implementing their suggestions. I am afraid that the independent tracks, many of which are very well run, will never join the NGRC structure, although they enjoy the benefits of the work done by that body, the race-days law and the lifting of the on-course betting tax being the obvious ones that spring to mind.

The upsurge in injuries to racing Greyhounds is causing great concern among caring owners and veterinary surgeons alike. Unfortunately many of the large tracks have closed and we have a situation where the remaining tracks and, indeed, the purpose-built ones are too sharp; the bends are not wide enough. Racing Greyhounds have come a long way in the last sixty years with regard to their increased speed, and some of the sharp tracks of today are quite unsuitable because the horrific corners put far too much strain on their legs. Managements cheerfully put six Derby-class dogs in a box, possibly with a total value at today's prices of £80,000–100,000, and then wonder why they have terrible crashes at the first bend. Moreover, they try to justify the accidents to boot.

It seems to us that on the sand tracks particularly the managements quite often get their maintenance wrong. We feel that in many cases there is not enough water put on and that they have a habit of rushing round with a harrow and then just rolling lightly. This then has the effect of making the sand loose and when the dogs are going round the bends they tend to slip. Many of the muscle injuries are collected that way as well as most of the incidents of wrist injuries.

We also feel that sand should be as firm and wet as it is on a beach when the tide has just gone out. We appreciate that it is very difficult to keep the dual surface tracks right when there is sand on the bends and grass on the straights. The main problem is that the sand tends to sink or get blown off and this then leaves a bump between the two surfaces. The sand in these cases has to be replaced very often and watered well all the time to encourage it to settle.

In a recent article that appeared in *The Sporting Life* Paddy Sweeney, the undisputed king of Greyhound veterinary surgeons and a true Greyhound man, suggested that breeders should try and breed a smaller type of Greyhound. This seems to be good sense; the tracks are not going to get any bigger, so the problem must be approached from a different angle if we are to reduce the increasing incidence of crippling injuries that these dogs suffer. It is indeed quite true that to have a fast Greyhound there is no need to have a monster. I remember when I handled Sand Star for the 1969 Derby, he only weighed 63 lbs (28 kg). Up to 68 or 70 lbs (30 or 31 kg) seems reasonable weight-wise, but over that, in the main, you do find that the dogs are more injury prone.

Owners are benefiting from increased prize money: the total paid out between track managements and sponsors in the first half of 1987 was up 9.2% on the same period in 1986. It is indeed time that the prize money was brought to a more realistic level, bearing in mind the price of Greyhounds and the scale of kennel fees. It still has a long way to go.

A nice thought to end this section with is that the Americans have honoured Ballyregan Bob with a superb trophy as All World Greyhound 1986. The last British Greyhound to receive an award from the Americans was Mick the Miller, who was elected to the Hall of Fame, the permanent museum and exhibition in Abilene.

9   Hints and Tips

The points in this section relate to things that perhaps we have for-gotten or that we have not given enough space to. Corns have been mentioned but perhaps not in enough detail, and they can be really an awful curse. Not only can they make the dog permanently lame, and to get rid of them costs in many instances quite a lot of money. Generally they can be avoided or at least the really bad ones can be. The cause is always a foreign body that works up into the pad. Grit or glass are the most common, and like the oyster with the pearl nature tries to protect the foot by growing something round it. In a great many cases the pads are worn very thin by too much road bashing. I feel that this mania for walking Greyhounds on the road for miles and miles is quite mad and also an utter waste of time.

If the problem is noticed soon enough there is a homoeopathic remedy called Thuga (200 potency), which if given the correct way is quite remarkable. The pills must, however, be used fresh and kept tightly corked, away from the air. To start the course you give one pill every six hours up to four times and thereafter one twice a day. It is a ten-day course and there are a few rules that have to be observed regarding administration. Always give them between meals and not near a meal time. The tablets must be crushed and dropped onto the back of the tongue. You will find that the pad starts to rise and the corn becomes quite visible and can be gently pulled out, root and all.

Now some people say that this treatment does not work. I wonder whether the reason is that the corn may have been left there too long and not noticed? Possibly the original cause of the corn, i.e. the piece of glass or grit, has worked its way right up into the foot and lodged somewhere near the joint of the toe. If the corn comes out and the dog continues to be lame the only answer is to X-ray the foot and try and find out whether this has in fact happened. There is an operation performed in Australia where the veterinary surgeon does not try to gouge the corn out but cuts straight across the pad and exposes the

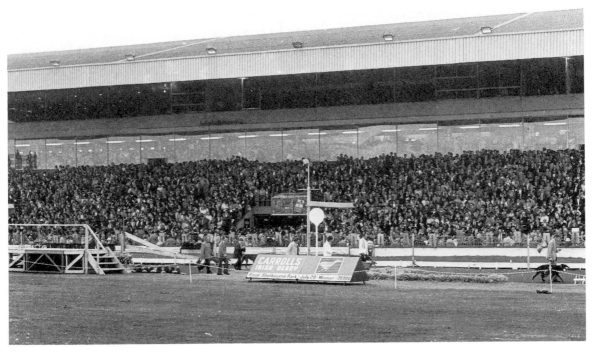

corn that way. Apparently the pad heals quite well and in many cases this operation is a success. I would think that it must be a last-ditch effort and should be avoided if possible.

Carroll's Derby Final night at Shelbourne Park, Dublin.

As stated in the section on minor injuries it is possible to get rid of corns with corn plasters and a solution that you paint on. One almost infallible way of diagnosing a corn, if you can't find anything else wrong, is to trot the dog up on a hard surface and he will be lame, and then try doing the same thing on grass and you will probably find him to be sound.

While we are on the subject of homoeopathic remedies, feverfew pills are really marvellous for arthritis. Like all health remedies you have to give them time. I give one tablet a day and keep the dog on them more or less all the time. After two or three weeks you will suddenly find that the joint, or whatever, no longer gives pain and the dog is sound. They work very well for old dogs who are quite often in considerable pain from some sort of rheumatism.

New Era make various biochemic salts for different complaints. They don't always work but can do no harm so are worth trying. I use Kali Sulph for dogs that tend to scratch and get skin problems that are not mange. Put these on the food and, again, you have to persevere with them. Make sure that you keep the pot properly sealed. Another very cheap and little-used product for blood disorders is flowers of sulphur. This is very effective and can be bought from a chemist. I daresay that because it is cheap in this day of high-cost drugs people think that it is no good. A weekly dose of this on the food usually keeps the blood clear and reduces the incidence of skin rashes. Kosolian, although made for horses, is a very good blood purifier also.

I use the biochemic salt that is suggested for cramp. This does work provided you are feeding your dog correctly and not pushing too much protein into the food, in other words giving a balanced diet. This problem of too much protein seems to be one of the main causes of cramp.

Another good homoeopathic remedy is arnica. This is used for muscle strain and bruising and does take the pain away. Comfrey oil also has many applications for rubbing on muscles and tendons; it relieves pain and keeps the area treated pliable. I ran a dog all through one Derby with a tendon. He got into the final complete with tendon, his comfrey oil and his holy water. Of course, the tendon had to be cut eventually but it did a good stand-by job.

It seems that dog owners do not understand about worming dogs. A man, who shall be nameless, recently told me that he had wormed his dog out, doubtless quite rightly. He also told me that he had run the dog at his permit track the following night and was surprised that his dog had lost a kilo in weight and finished last. I tried to explain that it is not a good thing to worm Greyhounds when they are down to run the next day, and that by so doing you run the risk of seriously affecting the dog's health and making it very susceptible to dehydration which, if left untreated, can have very dire consequences. Not only that but quite often the dog will get stomach cramp. Anyway, how would you like to be asked to run 500 yards if you had had the 'runs' the day before?

Just recently I have come across a liquid called Hydralex Silicone whose sole distributors are Associated Building Products Ltd. It is a damp-proofing product and it occurred to me that it might have an application on dog beds. I have tried it out successfully on a whelping box that we made at home. When applied to the surface and all the cracks, sides, front and back (in fact all over), it has the effect of making the board completely waterproof. If you pour water onto the surface it simply rolls off instead of soaking in. If one painted all the bottoms and fronts of the dog beds in the kennel with this it would save an enormous amount of aggravation when dogs wet the beds and cock their legs up the fronts. It would, I think, make dealing with wet beds a lot easier, and reduce the smell that is inevitable with this problem.

A word of warning though: I feel that the bed should be left for at least three days for the coating to dry out and for the smell to go off before putting dogs on.

If the case arises that you have a litter of pups that you wish to have reared, try and send them to an area where the subsoil is limestone or chalk. It seems that both dogs and horses reared on this type of land have stronger bone and do better.

Sometimes it happens that a dog has either been sick or is recovering from some complaint and refuses to eat. You are left with the problem of what to tempt him with. Try either kippers or sardines in oil. Up to today I have never had a dog refuse these foods.

Occasionally you will notice your dog trying to eat grass when out on the walk. That simply means that he needs vomiting out. It is nature's way of making a dog sick. If this happens, you should induce vomiting in the dog and you will be surprised at the amount of froth and yellow bile that is expelled. When I induce a dog to vomit I do it in the morning before breakfast. I give him about two cupfuls of milk and then about ten minutes later I put a lump of washing soda down his throat and take him into the yard, as near to a drain as possible. A few seconds' gently stroking his tummy upwards towards the back usually causes him to 'throw up'. As a matter of routine I usually do this about once a month, and I always do it before I worm the dogs. After about half an hour it is all right to give an ordinary breakfast.

Do remember that both rats and mice carry all sorts of disease. Always keep anything that you feed to the dogs securely shut up in bins so that rodents cannot get to it. There was a case not long ago where a trainer took over some kennels that were riddled with rats and mice and got in a rodent operator to kill them. The poison laid, in this case Warfarin, was hidden well away from where the dogs could reach it and the rodent population was being decimated slowly. However, during this operation the mice were walking around with the poison on their feet and as the dogs' bread was not being kept in bins, a very small amount of the poison was dropping off the mice onto the food. You would think that such a small amount would have no effect at all, but suddenly the dogs started to lose condition and became strangely lame in a joint for no apparent reason. The lameness would go away in about a week but then another dog would show the same symptoms. It took some time for this strange phenomenon to be understood but with the help of blood tests etc. it became clear what was happening.

Wherever there is food you will get mice and sometimes rats, but if the food is at all times kept secure and the cookhouse kept clean, so that bits of bread and so on don't get left lying around, there is hardly any chance of being overrun with rodents. They won't stay where there is nothing to eat. I keep and feed a troupe of wild cats here and this seems to keep the area outside pretty clear. Always feed cats if you want them to work.

It is important always to keep the inoculations for any retired dogs, stud dogs or breeding bitches up to date. You can never tell when something might be brought into the kennel or picked up at a track by the racing dogs and carried home. The dogs with their inoculations up to date will be immune from the problem but they can become carriers.

A good idea when feeding any of the expanded foods dry to a litter of pups that are running out in paddocks, is to put the food in a chicken hopper. It protects the food from getting wet and controls the amount that is dropped into the tray, so that the food can't get spoilt. It must be remembered that when you are feeding dry it is essential to always have water on tap.

Pups can get into a bad habit which will stay with them all their lives if it is not checked, of eating dog excreta. This is a filthy habit and can sometimes be traced to kennels or paddocks being left dirty. The first thing to help stop this habit from developing is to make sure that any excreta is picked up from the kennel and the paddocks regularly. When we have pups in for schooling I always go round after feeding and clean up the kennels or if the pups are turned out, weather permitting, the paddocks are routinely picked up before shutting up for the night.

Once this habit is formed it is very hard to eradicate. Various theories have been put forward about the dogs lacking some vitamin or other, and quite a good idea is to get some unprocessed tripe from the local slaughterhouse and feed that in the main meal with whatever else you are using. Giving plenty of minerals and vitamins might help also. But the main thing is to break the habit. I usually resort to keeping one of the Beaverwood muzzles on the dog and taping the front up so that he can't get anything through it. You have to persevere, though, but eventually it breaks the habit. The new era biochemic salt calc phos or calc carb is recommended for this problem.

When pups are about twelve months old they shed all their puppy coat and grow what will be their adult coat. Dogs moult every year but with pups it is a complete shed and at that time they need good doses of vitamins etc. to help them through this period. They tend to get a bit low and, if they are schooling at the time, they don't always do very well. They tend to lose weight and it is wise not to push them too hard until they are through this stage.

Another bad habit pups get into is turning in the traps. There are many ideas on how to stop them. One way is to have a single trap and fill in the inside with a piece of smooth plywood. It must be cut to fit all over one side of the inside of the trap with no cracks that the dog could get his foot stuck in. It needs to be thick enough to narrow the trap so that it makes it impossible for the dog to turn. Put the dog in and go round the front and talk to him for a few seconds, then let the lid up and let him out. Do this every day, increasing the time that you keep him in the box until he eventually becomes contented to stand there until he is let out. Ideally if you can take the trap to the schooling track and do this when he knows that the hare will be coming and that he is going to have a run, all the better. Sometimes it is the noise of the hare that starts off the turning habit. At other times it is just that the dog gets into the habit and when he has performed his antics and got round the right way again he will stand and wait for the hare like any other normal dog. It is, however, a habit to be deplored because in nine cases out of ten the dog will eventually hurt himself, the most common injuries being to put his pelvis out of line or to land on the point of his shoulder and bruise the bone badly.

I think I should mention foot fungus. It occurs mainly from wet paddocks where pups are reared and the kennel keepers lay straw down to try and dry the paddocks. This then produces the spores that cause the fungus. It also occurs in dirty kennels. Once you have it, getting rid of it is very difficult. Their are various anti-fungal preparations on the market, the most well known being Mycil cream for athlete's foot. If the condition has not got out of hand this can work. The anti-fungal pills, Flagyl or Griseofulvin, can also be effective. There is a product made by Willows Francis called Tenasol fungicidal spray which can be tried. I personally get some crystals that are dissolved in water and I soak the feet in the liquid every other day. I get these from Mrs Jones at the Dunton veterinary clinic (address in Appendix C) and they always clear up the most stubborn cases. I have never suffered from this problem here but quite a few of the pups that come in for schooling have the condition when they arrive.

It is possible, although not very usual, to have trouble with pups when they are teething. At about twelve weeks old the milk teeth fall out and the permanent teeth come through. Occasionally you may find that a pup goes off its food and loses condition. On inspecting the mouth, which is one of the first places to look if pups are not eating, you will find that the gums look sore and inflamed. There is not much that can be done apart from administering some aspirin twice a day

(ABOVE AND OPPOSITE)
Wimbledon Stadium.

and feeding the pup on soft food until the teeth come through. I
suppose it would be possible to try some of the preparations that are
currently rubbed on babies' gums when they are teething; that might
relieve the condition a bit.

Some pups are born with a cleft palate. When your vet comes to
check the bitch after whelping it's not a bad idea to have him look at
the pups for this. The sign indicating this condition is when the pup
does not seem to be sucking properly and the milk comes down its
nose. I am afraid they have to be put to sleep.

The question of suppressing oestrus in racing bitches has caused a

great deal of comment from many people within the sport. It has now been accepted by the NGRC that this practice is very common, but you are supposed to tell the racing manager that your bitch is on the 'pill' so that the information can be put on the race card.

However, there are various preparations used for this, one being the four-monthly injection of Delva Sterum, which is administered by the vet. Among the pills most currently used are Methyl Testosterone, or Primolute N. These pills are administered at the rate of one per day and it is usual to start the bitch on them one month before she is due to come in season. They can be continued for four to six weeks after her season date and then discontinued. Normally the bitch will not come into season at once so that you have about two months' extra running from her between seasons. I think these pills should only be used on bitches that break down every six months. Many Greyhound bitches will go nine or twelve months in between seasons, and I feel that they should be left alone and allowed to function in their proper cycle.

It is a bad thing to try and stop a season once it has started. It is possible but it ruins the form of the bitch and cannot in my opinion do her health any good. It is common practice in Ireland and America to start bitch puppies on an oestrus suppressant at about ten months old and not allow them to break down at all. Personally, I think that this is a mistake.

I very often get asked whether I think that these drugs affect the bitches when you want to breed from them. I feel that with the Delva Sterum injection it would be wise to allow the bitch to have one season clear before mating her on the second one. With the pill, if it is used as I have suggested, it seems to me that it would not interfere with her breeding potential and she could be mated on the season following the course of pills.

One final point: when a dog has a bandage, plaster or stitches, don't forget to put a box muzzle on him and keep it on apart from at feeding time. Dogs can destroy a plaster in about five minutes if they wish which will not make you popular with your veterinary surgeon.

Appendix A –
Food Products and Diet Sheets

Milk

LITTERLAC
Distributors
Volac Ltd
Orwell, Royston, Herts
Tel: 0223 208021

Vitamins guaranteed for 18 months from

Oil	30%
Protein	25.5%
Fibre	Nil
Ash	6%
Vit. A	50,000 iu/kg
Vit. D3	6,000 iu/kg
Vit. E	30 iu/kg
Vit. C	130 mg/kg
Thiamine (B1)	5.5 mg/kg
Riboflavin	20.0 mg/kg
Vit. B6	4.5 mg/kg
Vit. B12	50.0 mcg/kg
Nicotinic Acid	25.5 mg/kg
Choline	0.76 gm/kg
Calcium	8.60 gm/kg
Phosphorus	6.00 gm/kg
Magnesium	1.20 gm/kg
Sodium	4.20 gm/kg
Iron	80.00 mg/kg
Zinc	40.00 mg/kg
Manganese	20.00 mg/kg
Iodine	0.14 mg/kg
Lysine	1.6%
Methionine	0.5%

WHELPIE
Distributors
Vetbed Ltd
Oakenshaw Grange, Doncaster Road, Crofton,
Wakefield WF4 1SD
Tel: 0924 864970

Composition

Protein	27%
Fat	18%
Methionine	0.10%
Vitamin mixture	0.5%

Added Minerals
Calcium, Phosphorus, Magnesium, Iron, Copper, Manganese, Cobalt, Zinc, Sodium Iodide, Sodium Chloride

Added Vitamins
Vit. A   24,000 iu
Vit. D3   2,000 iu
Vit. E (25 mg) plus Vit. B, Vit. B2, Vit. B6, Vit. B4, Nicotinamide, Calcium Pantothenate, Choline Chloride, Vit. C

ANALYSIS OF MILK – BAINES 1981
Average analysis of milk as % (in brackets % dry matter)

	BITCH	COW	GOAT
Moisture	77.2	87.6	87.0
Dry Matter	22.8	12.4	13.0
Protein	8.1 (35.8)	3.3 (26.6)	3.3 (25.3)
Fat	9.8 (43.2)	3.8 (30.6)	4.5 (34.6)
Ash	4.9	5.3	6.2
Lactose	3.5 (15.2)	4.7 (37.9)	40.0 (30.8)
Calcium	0.28 (1.24)	0.12 (0.96)	0.13 (1.00)
Phosphorus	0.22 (1.01)	0.095 (0.76)	0.11 (0.84)
kcal/100 g	120	65	71

Supplements (for puppies)

STRESS
Distributors
Phillips Yeast Products Ltd
Park Royal, London

Analysis
Vit. A and D
Cobalt, Iodine, Zinc, Magnesium, Iron

Ash	60%
Calcium	15%

Phosphorus	12.5%
Sodium	1.5%
Magnesium	1.1%
Copper	83 mg
Vit. A	100,000 iu
Vit. D	10,000 iu/kg

PET-CAL
From Veterinary Surgeons Only
Each tablet contains
Dibasic Calcium Phosphate (Anhydrous) 2.04g
Supplying

Calcium	600 mg
Phosphorus	464 mg
Vit. D3	200 units

DUNLOP BONE MEAL
Distributors
W. & J. Dunlop Ltd
1–9 St Michael Street, Dumfries

Analysis

Nitrogen	4.9%
Protein	30.6%
Phosphoric Acid	21.1%

INTERVET (SA.37)
Distributors
Intervet Laboratories Ltd
Science Park, Milton Road, Cambridge CB4 4BH

Formula per 100 g

Vit. A	80,000 iu
Vit. D3	8,000 iu
Vit. E	1,000 iu
Vit. K3	280 mg
Vit. C	584 mg
Vit. B1	6.4 mg
Vit. B2	17.6 mg
Vit. B6	10 mg
Vit. B12	330 mg
Calcium	20 mg
Copper	125 mg
Cobalt	28 mg
Biotin	164 mcg

KOSSOLIAN
Distributors
Day, Son & Hewitt Ltd
10 Grant Street
Bradford 3, Yorks

Formula

Sodium Chloride	25.2%

Iron Sulphate	6.3%
Calcium Carbonate	6.3%
Iron Oxide	0.07%
Manganese Sulphate	160 ppm
Cobalt Sulphate	990 ppm
Potassium Iodide	65 ppm
Copper Sulphate	730 ppm
Calcium Phosphate	6.3%
Vit. B12	0.88 mcg

COOPO PRODUCTS Vitamin supplement
Distributors
Coopo Products Ltd
137 Malling Green, Lewes, Sussex BN7 2RB

Each gram contains

Vit. A	1,000 iu
Vit. D	100 iu
Vit. C	20 mg
Vit. E	2.5 iu
Vit. K	4.0 mg
Calcium Phosphate	5.0 mg
Copper	0.1 mg
Iodine	2.5 mg
Sodium Chloride	2.5 mg

AINTREE E1000 (for horses and dogs)
Distributors
Day, Son & Hewitt Ltd
St Georges Quay, Lancaster
Tel: 0524 381821

Contains

Oil	2.1%
Protein	10.8%
Fibre	2.7%
Ash	5.9%
Vit. E	45,000 iu/pg
Selenium	10 mg/kg

VITA – E.SUCCINATE
Distributors
Bioglan Laboratories Ltd
Hertford, Herts

Contains
Crystallina d. alphatocopheryl acid succinate, manufactured from natural sources, equivalent to 200 mg dl. alpha-tocopheryl acetate of 200, iu of Vit. E

LECTADE (oral rehydration therapy)
Distributors
Beecham Animal Health
Brentford, Middx

Ionix Constitution (mM per litre when dissolved)

Sodium	73.2
Potassium	15.6
Chloride	73.2
Citrate	1.4
Phosphate	15.0
Aminoacetic Acid	41.1
Dextrose	113.7

Foods

FEBO (Late Purina)
Distributors
Jenks Brokerage
Castle House
Desborough Road
High Wycombe
Bucks
Tel: 0494 33456

Typical Analysis
Puppy Food

Crude Protein	27.0%
Digestible Protein	21.6%
Crude Oil	11.0%
Crude Fibre	4.0%
Crude Ash	8.0%
Vit. A	5,000 ju/kg
Vit. D3	500 ju/kg
Vit. E	50 ju/kg

Greyhound Meal

Crude Protein	27.0%
Digestible Protein	21.6%
Crude Oil	12.0%
Crude Fibre	4.5%
Crude Ash	8.5%
Vit. A	5,000 ju/kg
Vit. D3	500 ju/kg
Vit. E	50 ju/kg

Dog Food

Crude Protein	22.0%
Crude Oil	11.0%
Crude Fibre	4.5%
Ash	7.0%
Vit. A	5,000 ju/kg
Vit. D3	500 ju/kg
Vit. E	50 ju/kg

Dog Meal

Crude Protein	25.0%
Crude Oil	11.0%
Crude Fibre	4.5%
Ash	7.5%
Vit. A	5,000 ju/kg
Vit. D3	500 ju/kg
Vit. E	

KASCO
Distributors
Kasco Consumer Relations
BP Nutrition (UK) Ltd
Stepfield
Witham
Essex CM8 3AB

Guaranteed Analysis
Mealettes

Crude Protein	27.0%
Crude Fibre	4.0%
Crude Fat	10.0%
Moisture	11.0%

WAFCOL
Distributors
Wafcol Ltd
Haigh Avenue
Stockport
Cheshire SK14 1NU

Guaranteed Analysis
Wafcol '20'

Protein	20%
Oil	6%
Ash	5%
Fibre	4%

Wafcol '24'

Protein	24%
Oil	6%
Ash	6%
Fibre	4%

Wafcol '27'

Protein	27%
Oil	8%
Ash	6%
Fibre	5%

High-Protein Puppy Meal

Protein	27%
Oil	8%
Ash	6%
Fibre	5%

High-Protein Racing Food

Protein	27%
Oil	8%
Ash	6%
Fibre	5%

Wafcol Greyhound Chunks

Protein	16%
Oil	6%
Ash	4%
Fibre	5%

CHALLENGE
Distributors
Volac Championship Food Ltd
Orwell
Royston
Herts SG8 5QX

Typical Analysis
Challenge High Protein

Oil	10%
Protein	31%
Fibre	4.5%
Ash	12.7%

Challenge Formula 3

Oil	6%
Protein	19%
Fibre	4%
Ash	7.6%

OMEGA
Distributors
Omega Pet Information Service
Edward Baker Ltd
Cornard Mills
Sudbury
Suffolk CO10 0JA
Tel: 0787 72353

Typical Analysis
Omega Complete Dog Food

Protein	24%
Oil	8%
Fibre	4.5%
Ash	8.5%
Vit. A	10,000 iu/kg
Vit. D3	1,500 iu/kg
Vit. E	50 mg/kg

SPRATTS

Distributors

Spratts Patent Ltd
New Malden House
1 Blagdon Road, New Malden,
Surrey
Tel: 01–949 6100 ext 272

Typical Analysis

Dog Diet 1 (for small dogs and puppies)
Dog Diet 2

Protein	25.0%
Oil	9%
Fibre	2.4%
Ash	10.6%
Vit. A	4,600 iu/kg
Vit. D3	460 iu/kg
Vit. E	46 mg/kg

BETA

Distributors

B.P. Nutrition
Customer Service Department
B.P. Nutrition (UK) Ltd
Wincham
Northwich
Cheshire CW9 6DF
Tel: 0606 41133

Typical Analysis

Beta Puppy

Protein	29%
Oil	10%
Fibre	3.5%

Beta Breeder

Protein	29%
Oil	8.5%
Fibre	3.5%

Beta Racer

Protein	29%
Oil	9%
Fibre	3%

EVENLODE

Distributors

Evenlode Products Ltd
Station Mills
Chipping Norton
Tel: 0608 2321

Calculated Analysis

Expanded Complete Puppy Food

Protein	27%
Oil	8%
Fibre	3.5%
Calcium	1.25%
Phosphorus	1.10%

Adult Expanded 25

Protein	25%
Oil	8%
Fibre	3.5%
Calcium	1.3%
Phosphorus	0.9%

Adult Expanded 18

Protein	18%
Oil	5%
Fibre	3.5%
Calcium	1.3%
Phosphorus	0.9%

LAUGHING DOG

Distributors

Roberts & Co. (Dunchurch) Ltd
London Road
Dunchurch, Nr. Rugby
Tel: 0788 810283

Typical Analysis

Laughing Dog Puppy Meal
Laughing Dog Terrier Meal

Protein	11.4%
Oil	1.6%
Fibre	2.7%
Calcium	0.4%
Phosphorus	2.6%
Carbohydrate	73.3%

Diet Sheet 1 (Puppies from fourteen days to six weeks)

I start puppies eating more or less as soon as their eyes open.

FIRST MEALS

Very small amounts of raw beef minced twice to break up the fibres.

To start pups, put scraps of mince on your finger and put gently in the mouth. Pups at this age suck it down. Then encourage the pups to suck their mother straight away. For the first day I do this just once. On the second day I do it twice. Most puppies, having had one taste of raw beef, will go mad when you arrive with the dish. It's no good putting the dish down on the bed because they try to suck the meat and splatter it everywhere.

Continue this exercise for a week, getting up to three small amounts each day.

WEEK 3

Early morning

Scramble some egg in the normal way and feed this from your hand. You will find it difficult to know which pup has had what when they are all the same colour, but I have a large box and as I feed I put each one down in the box. If you have any egg left give the second helping in the reverse, putting the fed pups back in the bed.

Mid-day

Small amounts of minced beef, still fed from the hand. Most pups stop being interested if they are full, so don't force them. However, use your common sense with the greedy ones as they tend to stuff themselves silly if you allow it.

Early evening
Small amounts of more mince or scrambled egg. It's not terribly important at this stage which you give them because they are still with the mother, and hopefully because you are helping her she will have a decent amount of milk.

WEEK 4
This is 'teaching-to-lap' week. Use flat pans without too much lip on; small roasting trays, old frying pans, or old grill pans are very good. Use something fairly heavy, otherwise they will put their feet on the edge and over will go the milk. Be warned: the first attempts at lapping mainly result in more milk on the outside of the pup than on the inside. Three pups to a dish is plenty to cope with if you are not to get smothered in milk as well.

Early morning
Lapping practice. Types of suitable milk will be found listed on page 121.

Mid-day
Raw minced beef. At this stage the food can be offered on a dish. Puppies do have a habit of getting food everywhere, so you will have to help them get the mince up by pushing it into little lumps with your finger.

Tea time
Scrambled egg, fairly milky, also in the dish. More mess – but most of it goes down eventually.

Evening
Drop of milk. You will find that the mother will clean the pups up very nicely for you after the messy feeds. Continue this system to the end of week 4.

WEEK 5
The bitch will not have much milk now so the amounts must be increased.

Early morning
Scrambled egg. Add a little crumbled brown bread to soak up the excess milk.
Minced meat moistened with some nice broth (not fatty).

3.00 pm
Same as noon.

6.00 pm
Scrambled egg with brown bread, same as early morning.

Late night (about 10.00 pm)
Drink of milk.

By this age the puppies should be eating well and the bitch won't have much milk. So you must increase the amounts of each feed to satisfy their appetite.

WEEK 6
Same as week 5 with increased amounts.
Start putting bone meal and Stress in one meat feed according to the instructions.
This diet can be altered sensibly at this age. Cereal can be given with the milk in the morning feed, and just one egg feed at 6 o'clock. One egg per puppy scrambled should be adequate, with small amounts of brown bread and extra milk added.
The reason for so many meals is to ensure that the pups don't get distended stomachs from eating too much at once.
This diet can be continued until twelve weeks with the inclusion of some cooked vegetables, except carrots, minced and added to the meat feeds.
A change can also be made to a good puppy meal, e.g. Laughing Dog, well soaked and added to the meat feeds about half and half.
At nine to ten weeks the number of meals can be cut to four. Taking out the 3.00 pm feed and extending the time to about 1.00 pm for the noon feed and 4.30 pm for the next one. This then eliminates the 6.00 pm feed. The 4.30 feed can be either meat etc. or scrambled egg on alternate days.

Diet Sheet 2 (Puppies from twelve weeks upwards)

Breakfast
1 pint (600 ml) of milk with two slices brown bread and one raw egg. The bread can be toasted or baked in the oven. To bake it in the oven is quite simple. When the oven is finished with after the cooking is done, put the bread on a baking tray and leave in the oven while it cools. That dries the bread off and makes it slightly brittle. Brown bread needs to stale in any case. The amount you feed has to be increased as the pup grows.

Mid-day
In the morning soak a good-quality puppy meal, enough for two feeds. I would think that two double handfuls would be ample for one pup for two feeds. The meal should be soaked in hot water for at least two hours. At mid-day divide the meal into two, saving half for the tea-time feed. Mix $\frac{1}{2}$ lb (250 g) good quality mince, either raw or cooked, with the meal and some vegetables. The vegetables should consist of greens, leeks, celery, parsnip, onions but not carrots. Carrots are very indigestible and pass through more or less as they went in. The vegetables can be varied and it is

not necessary to cook all of them every day. Keep the water from the meat if you cook it and be sure to save the vegetable water too, because a great deal of the goodness from the vegetables is in the water. This 'soup' can then be used to moisten the food. When feeding on this system the food needs to be fairly sloppy.

Tea-time

Same as mid-day.

Bedtime

A nice drink of milk. The pup will go to bed contented and you will have got the required amount of milk into it with no hassle.

This diet is only one way, and is, I might add, the old-fashioned way of feeding.

Always have clean water available.

Diet Sheet 3 (Puppies over twelve weeks being reared on high-protein expanded foods)

Morning

An egg beaten in 1 pint (600 ml) of milk with brown bread or brown bread toasted (baked in the oven).

Mid-day

A meal of 29% protein expanded food of your choice. This must be well soaked in very hot water for at least one and a half hours, or until you can squash the pellets completely with your fingers. Some extra soup can be added for taste and heat before feeding.

Tea-time

Same as mid-day.

Evening and Bedtime

Drink of milk, at least 1 pint (600 ml).

IMPORTANT POINTS TO REMEMBER WHEN FEEDING EXPANDED FOODS

If the food is not properly soaked the swelling/soaking process continues inside the dog's stomach. This then draws fluid from the dog's body to complete the process and can result in severe kidney damage. When using these foods make sure that there is a good supply of clean water always available.

This type of food can be fed dry, *ad lib*, left in a bowl for the pups to eat as they please. If this method is used the water supply is absolutely vital.

The amounts are stated on the bag according to the weight of the dog, but I feel that you should use your own discretion about this and, to start with, use more than the makers advise. Thereafter use your own judgment as to whether the pups are carrying enough weight or not. Remember, pups grow and will need increasing quantities as they get bigger.

Milk, more or less *ad lib* (the 2 pints (1 litre) a day I have suggested is really to start with), is essential until the pups are at least six months old.

Don't ever forget the water.

Appendix B –
Greyhound Racing Tracks

NGRC Tracks

(Licensed to operate under the Rules of the National Greyhound Racing Club). *All distances in metres*

ENGLAND AND SCOTLAND

Birmingham – Hall Green
Greyhound Racing Association Ltd
Hall Green Stadium
York Road
Hall Green
Birmingham B28 8LQ
Tel: 021 777 1181/4

Days of racing – Mondays, Wednesdays, Saturdays

Best Times

259	Fearless Action	15.46	30.11.85
474	Rikasso Hiker	28.59	13.10.82
464H	Lovely Pud	29.38	8.9.84
606	Glideaway Ted	38.78	27.3.82
663	Special Bran	41.50	7.9.85
815	Scurlogue Champ	52.51	1.12.84

Brighton & Hove
Brighton & Hove Stadium Ltd
Nevill Road
Hove
Sussex BN3 7BZ
Tel: 0273 204601

Days of racing – Mondays, Wednesdays, Thursdays, Saturdays

Best Times

285	Stop The Codding	16.75	12.7.86
515	Glen Miller	29.62	4.5.82
515H	Sir Winston	30.47	9.7.83
695	Ballyregan Bob	41.13	2.11.85
695H	August Monday	42.86	6.6.81
970	Sandy Lane	59.66	20.8.83

Bristol – Eastville   Bristol Greyhounds
Bristol Stadium plc
Stapleton Road
Bristol BS5 6NW
Tel: 0272 511919

Days of racing – Mondays, Wednesdays, Fridays, Saturdays

Best Times

266	Rapid Mover	16.26	21.3.87
470	Rolstone Silk	28.05	25.10.79
470H	Sharp Lookout	29.53	13.9.76
670	Rolstone Silk	41.39	18.6.81
874	Keem Princess	54.59	16.8.80

Cradley Heath
Cradley Heath Greyhound Stadium Ltd
Dudley Wood Road
Dudley
West Midlands DY2 0DH
Tel: 0384 66604

Days of racing – Tuesdays, Fridays

Best Times

272	Tea Punt	15.91	24.7.81
462	Slender Boy	28.12	8.11.83
647	Ballybeg Brand	40.35	28.9.77
692	Rita's Hero	42.40	23.4.82
875	Pineapple Choice	55.73	20.7.82

Crayford
Ladbroke Stadia Ltd
Stadium Way
Crayford
Kent DA1 4HR
Tel: 0322 522262

Days of racing – Mondays, Thursdays, Saturdays

Best Times

380	Landfair Lass	24.35	24.9.86
380H	Jeddah Lady	24.93	8.10.86
540	Clover Park	35.31	8.12.86
714	Venture Boy	47.70	1.9.86
874	Sneaky Liberty	59.86	1.9.86

Derby
Lochranda Limited
Derby Greyhound Stadium
Vernon Street
Derby DE1 1FR
Tel: 0332 44107

Days of racing – Mondays, Wednesdays, Saturdays

Best Times

246	Spiral Gigi	14.94	26.8.85
420	Bleakhall Wonder	25.74	5.5.86
590	Band of Joy	36.89	30.11.83
764	Scurlogue Champ	49.04	16.11.85
934	Sheffield Silver	61.95	15.4.85

Edinburgh – Powderhall
Greyhound Racing Association Ltd
Powderhall Stadium
Edinburgh EH7 4JE
Tel: 031 556 8141/2

Days of racing – Tuesdays, Thursdays, Saturdays

Best Times

241	Briarhill Don	14.55	8.8.87
465	Princes Pal	27.58	29.8.87
465H	Cavan Town	28.68	2.5.87
650	Carrigeen Bree	40.25	2.5.87
824	Water Cannon	52.86	29.8.87

Glasgow – Shawfield
Shawfield Greyhound Racing & Leisure
Group Ltd
Shawfield Stadium
Rutherglen
Glasgow
Lanarks G73 1SZ

Days of racing – Tuesdays, Thursdays, Saturdays

No best times available.

Hull
Hull Kingston Greyhound Stadium Ltd
Craven Park
Holderness Road
Hull HU9 3JA
Tel: 0482 74131

Days of racing – Thursdays, Saturdays

Best Times

265	Spiral Gigi	15.91	10.7.86
458	Inchy Sand	27.70	9.10.86
644	Black Lupin	40.22	29.1.87

London – Catford
Greyhound Racing Association Ltd
Catford Stadium
Catford Bridge
London SE6 4RJ
Tel: 01 690 2261

Days of racing – Mondays, Thursdays, Saturdays

Best Times

385	One to Note	23.54	11.5.85
385H	Ballaugh Echo	24.17	19.6.86
555	Track Man	34.47	22.9.84
555H	Castletons Cash	35.56	2.9.86
718	Scurlogue Champ	45.58	20.10.84
888	Scurlogue Champ	57.60	19.6.86
1051	Cregagh Prince	69.93	29.4.87

London – Hackney
Brent Walker Ltd
Hackney Stadium
Waterden Road
Stratford
London E15 2EQ
Tel: 01 986 3511

Days of racing – Tuesdays, Thursdays, Saturdays

Best Times

247	Ballygroman Jim	15.17	30.10.85
304	Clear Reason	18.02	1.3.75
484	London Spec	29.02	27.3.76
484H	Westpark Clover	30.28	6.3.84
523	Ballyregan Bob	31.07	11.12.84
523H	Breakaway Slave	32.87	10.4.82
683	Ballyregan Bob	42.24	16.11.85
740	Swift Duchess	45.83	11.11.82
920	My Tootsee	59.21	11.2.86

London – Walthamstow
Walthamstow Stadium Ltd
Chingford Road
London E4 8SJ
Tel: 01 531 4255

Days of racing – Tuesdays, Thursdays, Saturdays

Best Times

235	Barbaran	14.23	16.4.85
415	Roseville Fergie	25.06	18.6.87
475	Deal Joker	28.54	18.7.81
475H	Thanet Queen	29.89	3.7.81
640	Westmead Call	39.30	6.8.87
820	Todo's Lisa	51.58	7.10.69
880	Yankee's Shadow	55.99	11.10.86
1045	Silver Mask	67.37	9.6.87

London – Wembley
Wembley Stadium Ltd
The Empire Stadium
Wembley
Middlesex HA9 0DW
Tel: 01 902 8833

Days of racing – Mondays, Wednesdays, Fridays, Saturdays

Best Times

275	Often Hungry	16.06	13.8.86
490	Fearless Champ	28.89	11.4.86
490H	Castletons Cash	29.70	28.4.86
655	Ballyregan Bob	39.46	23.8.85
655H	Ellas Ivy	40.99	14.8.87
710	Ballyregan Bob	42.63	11.12.85
850	Pineapple Choice	52.53	26.7.82

London – Wimbledon
Greyhound Racing Association Ltd
Wimbledon Stadium
Plough Lane
London SW17 0BL
Tel: 01 946 5361

Days of racing – Tuesdays, Thursdays, Saturdays

Best Times

252	Desert Moth	15.08	10.12.82
412	Ballinahow Lou	24.89	27.12.84
460	Fearless Action	27.47	14.12.85
480	Lodge Prince	28.34	29.5.86
660	Ballyregan Bob	40.15	19.4.86
660H	Longcross Bruce	41.52	6.8.82
820	Star Decision	51.48	28.7.84

	Glenowen Queen	51.48	28.12.83
868	Sandy Lane	54.11	6.5.83

Maidstone
Todos Promotions Ltd
Maidstone Greyhound Stadium
London Road
Maidstone
Kent ME16 0DT
Tel: 0622 674024/5

Days of racing – Tuesdays, Fridays, Saturdays

Best Times

454	Westmead Wish	28.21	21.11.86
644	Myarny	41.16	26.4.83
850	Malibu Light	54.38	7.10.83

Manchester – Belle Vue
Greyhound Racing Association Ltd
Belle Vue Greyhound Racecourse
Kirkmanshulme Lane
Gorton
Manchester M18 7BA
Tel: 061 223 1266

Days of racing – Tuesdays, Thursdays, Saturdays

Best Times

250	Nights Runner	14.37	9.5.87
460	Fearless Action	27.50	27.9.86
460H	Bewitching Test	29.34	15.3.86
645	Glenbrian Smut	40.08	28.9.85
815	Laden Jenny	52.30	15.9.84
853	Scurlogue Champ	54.62	28.9.85

Middlesbrough
National Greyhounds (Middlesbrough) Ltd
Cleveland Park Stadium
Stockton Road
Middlesbrough
Cleveland TS5 4AE
Tel: 0642 2473811

Days of racing – Wednesdays, Saturdays

Best Times

266	Lincolns Inn	16.18	24.7.71
282H/C	Sutton Black	17.11	2.5.84
462	Malaria	27.96	6.7.68
478H/C	Lucky Saint	29.25	11.6.83
640	Claudyne	39.75	11.8.65
656H/C	Liverton Rose	41.26	6.10.84
847	Ryehope Dawn	55.90	27.5.85

Newcastle – Brough Park
Brough Park Greyhounds Ltd
Brough Park Stadium
The Fossway
Newcastle-Upon-Tyne NE6 2XJ
Tel: 0632 658011

Days of racing – Tuesdays, Thursdays, Saturdays

Best Times

290	Meadowbank Snooker	17.38	6.10.83
460	Templemartin Una	28.00	11.10.86
460H/C	Pond Pikasso	28.46	6.8.85
500	Moneypont Coal	30.08	12.10.85
500H	Face the Mutt	31.43	1.7.82
670	Ballyregan Bob	41.15	8.5.86
670H/C	Gries Emperor	42.06	24.9.83
825	Scurlogue Champ	52.62	11.6.85

Nottingham
Colwick Park Sports Stadium
Colwick Park
Nottingham NG2 4BE
Tel: 0602 598231

Days of racing – Tuesdays, Thursdays, Saturdays

Best Times

312	Parkers Moon	18.61	4.10.84
485	Myrtown Best	29.56	4.12.80
485H	Keem Flower	30.28	11.7.81
500	Rock the Boat	30.43	12.9.85
500H	Speedy Tiger	30.99	17.10.85
530	Decoy Gold	32.03	16.10.80
680	Ballyregan Bob	41.87	9.11.85
754	Change Guard	47.02	3.6.87

Oxford
Northern Sports (Oxford) Ltd
Oxford Stadium
Sandy Lane
Cowley
Oxford OX4 5LJ
Tel: 0865 778222

Days of racing – Tuesdays, Thursdays, Saturdays

Best Times

250	Hardy Man	15.10	6.4.86
450	Parkers Sage	26.89	28.9.85
450H	Burgess Rocket	27.87	5.10.85
645	Run Free	39.46	11.11.86
845	Jaroadel	52.91	3.8.86

Poole
TGV Ltd
Poole Stadium
Wimbourne Road
Poole
Dorset BH15 2BH
Tel: 0202 674218

Days of racing – Thursdays, Saturdays

Best Times

232	Seaman's Hope	14.41	25.4.85
455	Golden Sand	27.34	30.8.83
632	Farmhill Jill	40.00	25.9.86
855	Scurlogue Champ	54.86	12.7.86

Portsmouth
Greyhound Racing Association Ltd
Portsmouth Stadium
Target Road
Tipnor
Portsmouth
Hants PO2 8QU
Tel: 0705 663232

Days of racing – Tuesdays, Fridays, Saturdays

Best Times

256	Sir Gaylord	15.77	16.11.84
438	Skelleg's Tiger	26.63	19.7.85
610	Wellington Lad	38.32	16.10.84
792	Airmount Sand	50.65	16.10.84

Ramsgate
Northern Sports (Ramsgate) Ltd
Ramsgate Stadium
Hereson Road
Dumpton Park
Ramsgate
Kent CP11 7EU
Tel: 0843 593333

Days of racing – Wednesdays, Saturdays

Best Times

450	Creamery Cross	26.96	2.7.83
640	General Leader	40.01	26.9.83
855	Glenowen Queen	53.95	2.12.85
1045	Belladere	68.60	19.5.86

Reading
Allied Presentations Ltd
Reading Stadium
Bennet Road
Smallmead
Reading
Berks RG2 0JL
Tel: 0734 863161

Days of racing – Thursdays, Saturdays

Best Times

275	Greenfield Fox	16.32	23.10.82
465	Hillville Flyer	28.13	16.12.82
465H	The Dingle Man	28.93	8.1.83
660	Astrosyn Doll	41.14	19.11.83
660H	Trixie's Snipe	42.51	19.11.83
850	Jo's Gamble	54.50	19.11.83
1045	Simply Sweet	70.54	1.11.86

Romford
Romford Stadium Ltd
London Road
Romford
Essex RM7 9DU
Tel: 0708 762345

Days of racing – Mondays, Tuesdays, Saturdays

Best Times

400	Sado's Choice	23.87	6.12.86
400H	Barrymoss Queen	24.50	8.8.85
575	Bermudas Fun	35.15	11.7.78
	Ballyregan Bob	35.15	9.7.85
575H	Champagne Glory	36.22	16.10.84
715	Scurlogue Champ	44.18	16.10.84
750	Keem Rocket	46.70	2.3.85
925	Salina	59.13	7.4.81
1100	Tartan Sarah	73.15	5.3.85

Sheffield
Sheffield Sports Stadium Ltd
The Stadium
Penistone Road
Owlerton
Sheffield S6 2DE
Tel: 0742 343074

Days of racing – Tuesdays, Fridays, Saturdays

Best Times

290	Fearless Prince	16.78	13.8.80
380	Loughlass Champ	22.09	8.2.80
500	Desert Pilot	29.38	25.4.80

650	Desert Pilot	38.80	9.8.80
715	White Rooms	43.78	27.6.80
730	Beano Blondie	44.63	22.8.86
800	Change Guard	49.02	15.8.86

Swindon
Abbey Stadium Ltd
Blunsdon
Nr. Swindon
Wilts SN2 4ND
Tel: 0793 721333

Days of racing – Mondays, Wednesdays, Fridays

Best Times

275	Fearless Swift	16.28	19.8.85
480	Looney Bill	28.26	18.10.82
	Peasdown Julie	28.26	9.11.83
510	Westmead Gold	29.98	1.7.87
685	Black Port	41.72	18.7.84
730	Go Go Tiger	45.37	17.6.85
943	Tartan Sarah	58.52	23.7.84

Wolverhampton
Ladbroke Stadia Ltd
Monmore Green Stadium
Sutherland Avenue
Monmore Green
Wolverhampton WV2 2JJ
Tel: 0902 56663

Days of racing – Tuesdays, Thursdays, Saturdays

Best Times

277	Fearless Champ	16.34	9.11.85
462	Fearless Champ	28.12	18.1.86
484	Fearless Power	29.26	8.11.86
484H	Rusty Prince	30.69	28.8.82
647	Telecom Tiger	40.42	18.10.86
815	Scurlogue Champ	51.64	22.5.85
900	Make It Hot	58.05	5.11.83

Permit Licensed Racecourses

Canterbury
Kingsmead Stadium
Kingsmead Road
Canterbury
Kent CT2 7PH
Tel: 0227 61244

Days of racing – Tuesdays, Fridays

Best Times

400	Westwood Hoe	25.45	29.9.87
	Bluefalls Boy	25.45	2.10.87
578	Bedemar Zelda	37.15	18.9.87

Henlow
Bedford Stadiums Ltd
Henlow Greyhound Stadium
Bedford Road
Lower Standon
Henlow
Beds
Tel: 0462 813608

Days of racing – Mondays, Fridays

Best Times

318	Ecins Best	19.01	8.9.80
484	Westmead Call	29.12	10.10.86
730	Blue Shirt	45.50	18.6.84
890	Cregagh Prince	57.29	23.3.87

Ipswich
Ipswich Stadium Ltd
London Road
Ipswich
Suffolk IP1 2EJ
Tel: 0473 53337

Days of racing – Wednesdays, Saturdays

Best Times

258	Night Runner	15.15	4.6.86
440	Swift Rapier	26.48	4.9.82
628	Choice Rock	38.39	10.11.82
810	Scurlogue Champ	51.44	19.9.84

Milton Keynes
Milton Keynes Stadium Ltd
Ashland
Bletchley
Milton Keynes MK6 4AN
Tel: 0908 670150

Days of racing – Thursdays, Saturdays

Best Times

245	Westfield Earl	14.76	24.8.78
440	Siroco	26.56	22.3.84
620	Glenowen Queen	38.11	8.8.85
815	Grangeglen Sam	51.73	8.9.84

Norton Canes
Extrasprint Ltd
Norton Canes Greyhound Stadium
Brownhills Road
Norton Canes
West Midlands WS8 7NB
Tel: 0543 77445

Days of racing – Mondays, Wednesdays, Fridays

Best Times

265	Adam	15.01	7.6.86
440	Oakfield Colin	26.91	18.11.83
617	Slaneyside Point	39.61	12.9.83

Peterborough
Peterborough Sports Stadium Ltd
First Drove
Fengate
Peterborough
Cambs PE1 5BJ
Tel: 0733 43788

Days of racing – Tuesdays, Thursdays, Saturdays

Best Times

235	Ports Delight	14.46	24.9.83
420	Townview Spring	25.58	29.4.86
605	Decoy Lassie	37.71	4.4.85
790	Aidans Choice	50.32	27.9.83

Rye House
Rye House Stadium
Rye Road
Hoddesdon
Herts EN11 0EH
Tel: 0992 464200

Days of racing – Wednesdays, Saturdays

Best Times

281	Daleys Gold	16.59	28.9.85
484	Glamour Hobo	29.25	12.11.85
670	Go Go Tiger	42.12	16.10.85
870	Cloonty Lib	57.05	2.10.85

Swaffham
Swaffham Greyhound Stadium
M.K. Breckland Promotions Ltd
Downham Road
Swaffham
Norfolk

Days of racing – Mondays, Fridays
No best times available at present.

Yarmouth
Norfolk Greyhound Racing Co Ltd
Yarmouth Stadium
Yarmouth Road
Caister-on-Sea
Norfolk NR30 5TE
Tel: 0493 720343

Days of racing – Tuesdays, Saturdays

Best Times

277	Knockrour Brandy	16.64	22.9.79
462	Ramtogue Dasher	27.91	9.9.87
659	Dunmurry Girl	40.88	3.8.72
843	Change Guard	53.62	20.8.86
1041	Dunmurry Ruby	69.15	6.12.86

Tracks in Ireland

Telephone numbers are Irish national numbers and should be prefixed by the appropriate international code when dialling direct from Britain. Exceptions are the Northern Ireland tracks where the STD direct-dial codes are included. Track surfaces are grass or grass and sand. Major exceptions are the all-sand circuits at Dungannon, Dunmore and Clonmel. Outside hares are the norm. All distances are metric for the first time: 525 yards is 480 metres; 550 yards is 503 metres; 700 yards is 640 metres.

Clonmel
Davis Road
Clonmel
Tel: 052 21118
Distances – 274, 480, 503, 640 metres
Days of racing – Mondays, Thursdays

Cork
Western Road
Cork
Tel: 021 43013
Distances – 274, 480, 640, 681 metres
Days of racing – Mondays, Wednesdays, Saturdays

Derry
Brandywell
Derry
Tel: 0504 65461
Distances – 274, 457, 480, 549, 658, 841 metres
Days of racing – Mondays, Fridays

Dundalk
Ramparts
Dundalk
Co. Louth
Tel: 042 34113

Distances – 293, 457, 480, 503, 640, 695 metres
Days of racing – Mondays, Fridays, Saturdays

Dungannon
Oaks Park
Dungannon
Co. Tyrone
Tel: 086 87 22023
Distances – 297, 457, 480, 503, 549, 713 metres
Days of racing – Wednesdays, Thursdays, Saturdays

Dunmore
Antrim Road
Belfast
Tel: 0232 776232
Distances – 329, 375, 398, 480, 503, 526, 549, 640 metres
Days of racing – Mondays, Tuesdays, Thursdays, Saturdays

Enniscorthy
The Showgrounds
Enniscorthy
Tel: 054 33172
Distances – 480, 503, 549 metres
Days of racing – Mondays, Thursdays

Galway
College Road
Galway
Tel: 091 62273
Distances – 297, 480, 503, 640, 740 metres
Days of racing – Tuesdays, Fridays

Harolds Cross
Harolds Cross Stadium
Dublin 6
Tel: 01 971081
Distances – 302, 480, 503, 530, 686, 759, 937 metres
Days of racing – Tuesdays, Thursdays, Fridays

Kilkenny
St James Park
Kilkenny
Tel: 056 21214
Distances – 274, 480, 640 metres
Days of racing – Wednesdays, Fridays

Lifford
Lifford
Co. Donegal
Tel: 0504 883523
Distances – 297, 480, 526, 722 metres
Days of racing – Tuesdays, Thursdays, Saturdays

Limerick
Markets Field
Limerick
Tel: 061 45170
Distances – 274, 480, 503, 640 metres
Days of racing – Mondays, Thursdays, Saturdays

Longford
Park Road
Longford
Tel: 043 45501
Distances – 302, 480, 503, 521, 549 metres
Days of racing – Mondays, Fridays

Mullingar
Ballinderry
Mullingar
Co. Westmeath
Tel: 044 48348
Distances – 297, 480, 503, 549, 736 metres
Days of racing – Tuesdays, Saturdays

Navan
Limekiln Hill
Trim Road
Navan
Co. Meath
Tel: 046 21739
Distances – 320, 480, 503, 549 metres
Days of racing – Wednesdays, Thursdays

Newbridge
Newbridge
Co. Kildare
Tel: 045 31270
Distances – 274, 480, 503, 549 metres
Days of racing – Mondays, Fridays

Shelbourne Park
Shelbourne Park
Dublin 4
Tel: 01 683502
Distances – 329, 480, 503, 526, 549, 686 metres
Days of racing – Mondays, Wednesdays, Saturdays

Thurles
Townspark
Thurles
Tipperary
Tel: 0504 21003
Distances – 302, 480, 503, 526, 549, 640, 768 metres
Days of racing – Tuesdays, Saturdays

Tralee
Kingdon Track
Tralee
Co. Kerry
Tel: 066 24033
Distances – 298, 480, 503, 521, 686, 742 metres
Days of racing – Tuesdays, Wednesdays, Fridays

Waterford
Kilcoham Park
Waterford
Tel: 051 74531
Distances – 274, 480, 503, 640, 704, 731 metres
Days of racing – Tuesdays, Saturdays

Youghal
Youghal
Co. Cork
Tel: 024 92305
Distances – 298, 480, 503, 640, 722 metres
Days of racing – Tuesdays, Fridays

TRACK RECORDS IN IRELAND
(Irish distances in yards)

Clonmel

300	Quiet Spring	16.50
500H	Knockdrina Ranger	29.95
500	Odd Venture	28.25
525H	Mars Mist	30.12
525	Balalika	28.68
550	Path Of Sand	30.52
730	Yellow Emperor	41.60
1000	Tokio Lady	58.99

Cork

300	Odell Supreme	16.43
310	Odd Crest	17.20
500	Prince Of Bermuda	27.95
525H	Race Riot	29.75
525	The Stranger	28.95
550	Spanish Lad	31.00
700	Anner Duke	39.80
745	Experience	42.80

Dundalk

320	Dark Landing	17.82
325H	Boston Heather	18.89
325	Mourne Return	17.85
500H	Tivoli Valley	29.26
500	Nubeika Aoikki	28.22
525H	Master Bob	30.42
525	Chief Ironside	29.30
550H	Pick Me	31.90
550	Disco Clare	30.72
700	Twelfth Man	40.20

760	Malachy's Well	44.38	525	Trip To Arran	29.10
	Jenny's Lot	44.38	550	Midland Bran	30.50
765	Full Book	44.48	600	Choice Model	32.92

Dunmore

360	Artie's Rover	19.71
410	Betune Road	22.26
435	Curryhill's Fox	23.11
525	Drapers Autumn	29.19
550	Gangster's Doll	30.54
575	Low Sail	32.54
600	Ballydonnel Sam	33.53
	Janet's Pulsar	33.53
700	Westpark Quail	39.13

Harolds Cross

330	Bray Vale	17.76
480	Nelson's Pillar	26.80
525H	Ring Cortnadi	29.78
525	Where's Carmel	28.78
550	Son Of Silver	30.46
580H	Dark Cowboy	32.88
580	Rail Ship	31.82
750	Azuri	42.00
830	Donore Boy	47.00
1025	I'm A Cooper	59.58

Enniscorthy

525	Milebush Swiftie	29.15
550	Tinnock Supreme	30.40
600	Just It	33.35
	Dryland Sailor	33.35

Kilkenny

300	Verboden	16.50
	Moygara Sligo	16.50
	Margoe's Choice	16.50
525	Lax Law	28.98
700	Glen Grange	40.67

Galway

325	The Quiffer	17.79
525	New Line Bridge	29.46
550	Olly's Mist	30.74
810	Deerwood	46.60

Lifford

325	Cooma Slave	17.67
525	Erin's Eye	29.09
	Slaney Stan	29.09
	Moss Chimes	29.09
550	Bowe Princess	31.08
575	Tour Valley	32.11
780	Bowe Princess	45.10
790	Barrack Maid	45.03

Limerick

300	Fionntra Favour	16.34
525H	Silver Light	30.10
525	Grove Whisper	29.06
550	Moran's Beef	30.06
700	Dromlara Champ	39.75

Newbridge

300	Clane Mint	16.50
525H	Moreen Flamingo	30.08
525	Some Skinomage	29.02
	Wise Band	29.02
550	Blue Baron	30.50
600	Curryhills Popsy	33.08

Longford

330H	Cave View Clipper	19.48
330	Cast No Stones	18.22
	Tubbercurry Lad	18.22
525H	Fortwilliam Pagan	31.44
525	Sampson Flash	29.28
550	Gary's Pet	30.98
570	Angel Wonder	32.85
600	Danba	34.67

Shelbourne Park

360	Lauragh Six	19.33
525H	Sand Blinder	29.46
525	Tantallon's Gift	28.73
550	Wise Band	30.23
550*	Lodge Prince	30.03
575	Noisy Party	31.74
600	Lazy Tim	33.07
750H	Waverley Supreme	42.39

* (525 traps)

Mullingar

300	Kilmagoura Again	17.00
325H	Fado	19.06
325	Greenhill Boxer	18.44
525H	Lodge Walk	30.62
525	Rex Again	29.55
550H	Kidge Walk	32.16
550	Murray's Mixture	30.88
600	Butterfly Billy	33.61
780	Little Ice	46.39

Thurles

330H	Rambler Tonic	18.80
330	Top Customer	18.04
525H	Special	29.75

Navan

350	Never So Gay	19.04

525	Sailing Weather	29.20
550	Inchon's Best	30.68
	Bucks Bran	30.68
575	Gastrognome	31.76
700	Orwell Wonder	40.00
840	Clanboy	48.16

Tralee

325	Glamour Hobo	17.86
525H	Ballyard Hurdler	29.85
525	Court Rain	28.90
550	Realting Best	30.40
570	Sirius	31.34
750	Slow Motion	42.40

Waterford

300	Tom's Pal	16.35
525H	I'm Funny	30.30
525	The Other Duke	29.24
700	Westpark Eve	40.10
770	Tain Nua	44.02

Youghal

325	Lough Tan	17.48
525	Glenpark Dancer	28.90
550	Lispopple Tiger	30.20
700	Blondie Brown	39.68
790	Fen Tiger	44.92

Non-NGRC Tracks
(all distances in yards)

SCOTLAND

Armadale
Bathgate
West Lothian
Tel: 0501 30803
Inside hare. Distances – 330, 540 yds
Days of racing – Mondays, Thursdays

Ashfield
404 Hawthorn Street
Glasgow 22
Tel: 041 336 8552
Inside hare. Distances – 270, 450, 640, 830 yds
Days of racing – Mondays, Wednesdays, Fridays

Auchinleck
Pennylands Road
Auchinleck
Nr. Cumnock
Tel: 0290 21777
Inside hare. Distances – 264, 410, 610 yds
Days of racing – Wednesdays, Saturdays

ENGLAND
NORTH EAST

Ashington
Portland Park
Ashington
Northumberland
Tel: 091 251 4812
Inside hare. Distances – 280, 470, 660 yds
Days of racing – Tuesdays, Fridays

Easington
Moorfield Stadium
Sunderland Road
Easington
Co. Durham
Tel: 0783 270256
Ball hare. Distances – 270, 460, 525, 640 yds
Days of racing – Thursdays, Saturdays

Gosforth
County Rugby Ground
Gosforth
Tyneside
Tel: 091 285 3144
Inside hare. Distances – 277, 480, 614, 680, 883 metres

Hartlepool
Clarence Road
Hartlepool
Cleveland
Tel: 0429 72283
Inside hare. Distances – 266, 460, 640 yds
Days of racing – Tuesdays, Fridays

Pelaw Grange
Drum Road
Chester-le-Street
Co. Durham
Tel: 091 410 2141
Inside hare. Distances – 270, 445, 630, 805 yds
Days of racing – Mondays, Thursdays, Saturdays

Skegness
The Stadium
Marsh Lane
Orby
Lincs
Tel: 0754 810457
Inside hare. Distances – 268, 452, 630 metres
Days of racing – Wednesdays

Spennymoor
Merrington Lane
Spennymoor
Co. Durham
Tel: 0388 815576

Inside hare. Distances – 300, 500, 700 yds
Days of racing – Thursdays, Saturdays

Stanley
Murray Park
Stanley
Nr. Consett
Tel: 0207 232711
Inside hare. Distances – 275, 450, 635, 820 yds
Days of racing – Mondays, Fridays, Saturdays

Sunderland
Newcastle Road
Sunderland
Tel: 0783 367250
Inside hare. Distances – 243, 420, 600, 777 metres
Days of racing – Mondays, Saturdays

Wheatley Hill
Wheatley Hill Stadium
Co. Durham
Tel: 0385 852751
Outside McGee hare. Distances – 285, 470, 615 yds
Days of racing – Wednesdays, Fridays

NORTH WEST

Barrow
Park Road Stadium
Barrow-in-Furness
Tel: 0229 64848
Inside hare. Distances – 250, 415, 595 metres
Days of racing – Tuesdays, Fridays

Blackpool
Princess Street
Blackpool
Lancs
Tel: 0253 22057
Outside hare. Distances – 250, 422, 593 metres
Days of racing – Mondays, Wednesdays, Fridays

Bolton
Raikes Park
Manchester Road
Bolton
Lancs
Tel: 0204 25181
Inside hare. Distances – 313, 535, 745, 980 yds
Days of racing – Mondays, Wednesdays, Saturdays

Chester
Sealand Road
Chester
Tel: 0244 371572
Inside hare. Distances – 292, 489, 685 metres
Days of racing – Mondays, Saturdays

Oldham
Watersheddings
Oldham
Lancs
Tel: 061 624 1343
Inside hare. Distances – 240, 420, 585, 767 yds
Days of racing – Tuesdays, Thursdays, Saturdays

Preston
Acregate Lane
Preston
Lancs
Tel: 0772 794912
Inside hare. Distances – 255, 425, 610, 780 metres
Days of racing – Tuesdays, Thursdays, Saturdays

St Helens
Park Road
St Helens
Lancs
Tel: 0744 23346
Inside hare. Distances – 275, 490, 680 yds
Days of racing – Tuesdays, Fridays

Westhoughton
Wigan Road
Westhoughton
Tel: 0942 55207
Inside hare. Distances – 280, 450, 650, 825 yds
Days of racing – Mondays, Thursdays, Fridays

Winsford
Winsford United Football Stadium
Winsford
Tel: 06065 58325
Inside hare. Distances – 276, 476, 665 metres
Days of racing – Tuesdays, Thursdays

Workington
West Cumberland Stadium
Lonsdale Park
Workington
Tel: 0900 2464
Inside hare. Distances – 320, 530, 755 yds
Days of racing – Mondays, Saturdays

YORKSHIRE

Askern
Selby Road
Askern
Nr. Doncaster
Tel: 0302 701550
Inside hare. Distances – 285, 480, 660 metres
Days of racing – Wednesdays, Saturdays

Barnsley
Dillington Park
Barnsley
Tel: 0226 283860
Inside hare. Distances – 240, 368, 462, 600 metres
Days of racing – Wednesdays, Fridays

Highgate
Nicholas Lane
Goldthorpe
Rotherham
Tel: 0709 895364
Inside hare. Distances – 260, 304, 414, 590, 630, 740 metres
Days of racing – Mondays, Thursdays, Saturdays

Kinsley
Wakefield Road
Kinsley
Nr. Pontefract
Tel: 0977 610946
Inside hare. Distances – 260, 460, 630 metres
Days of racing – Tuesdays, Saturdays

Whitwood
Whitwood Greyhound Stadium Ltd
Altofts Lane
Whitwood
Castleford
West Yorkshire.
Tel: 0977 559940
No distances available
Days of racing – Mondays, Fridays

MIDLANDS

Chasewater
Pool Road
Brownhills
Staffs
Tel: 0543 375092
Outside hare. Distances – 290, 450, 700 metres
Days of racing – Tuesdays, Thursdays

Chesterfield
Chesterfield Sports Stadium
Station Road
Brimington
Tel: 0246 32516
Inside hare. Distances – 100, 290, 358, 452, 500, 700 yds
Days of racing – Mondays, Wednesdays, Fridays

Chesterton
Loomer Road
Chesterton
Newcastle-under-Lyme
Tel: 0782 562184
Outside hare. Distances – 272, 425, 469, 673, 864 metres
Days of racing – Wednesdays, Fridays

Coalville
Belvoir Road
Coalville
Leics
Tel: 021 351 2973
Outside hare. Distances – 300, 500, 700, 900 yds
Days of racing – Tuesdays, Saturdays

Cobridge
Waterloo Road
Cobridge
Stoke-on-Trent
Tel: 0782 279546
Outside hare. Distances – 270, 470, 670, 870 metres
Days of racing – Mondays, Saturdays

Hinckley
Nutts Lane
Hinckley
Leics
Tel: 0455 634006
Inside hare. Distances – 300, 500, 700 yds
Days of racing – Mondays, Wednesdays, Saturdays

Long Eaton
Station Road
Long Eaton
Notts
Tel: 0602 733494
Inside hare. Distances – 300, 485 metres
Days of racing – Tuesdays, Fridays

Warwick
Emscote Road (rear Pottertons)
Warwick
Tel: 0926 495223
Outside hare. Distances – 275, 450, 610, 810 metres
Days of racing – Thursdays, Saturdays

WALES

Bedwellty
Bedwellty Stadium
Bargoed
South Wales
Tel: 0443 831072

Inside hare. Distances – 310, 510, 700 yds
Days of racing – Mondays, Saturdays

Skewen
Winifred Road
Skewen
Tel: 0792 812469
Inside hare. Distances – 312, 530, 760 yds
Days of racing – Wednesdays, Fridays

Swansea
Ystrad Road
Fforestfach
Swansea
Tel: 0792 812469
Inside hare. Distances – 312, 525, 730 yds
Days of racing – Tuesdays, Saturdays

Valley
Tredomen Athletic Stadium
Ystrad
Mynach
Tel: 0443 813529
Inside hare. Distances – 310, 515, 700 yds
Days of racing – Tuesdays, Thursdays

SOUTH WEST

Exeter
County Ground
Exeter
Devon
Tel: 0392 73132
Inside hare. Distances – 250, 440, 620 metres
Days of racing – Tuesdays, Fridays

Glastonbury
Godney Road
Glastonbury
Somerset
Tel: 027 875 232
Outside hare. Distances – 280, 475, 700, 895 metres
Days of racing – Tuesdays, Fridays

Newton Abbot
The Racecourse
Newton Abbot
Devon
Tel: 0626 51183
Inside hare. Distances – 325, 482, 525, 762 yds
Days of racing – Wednesdays, Saturdays

St Austell
Cornish Stadium
Par Moor
St Austell
Cornwall
Tel: 0726 850224
Inside hare. Distances – 250, 450, 650, 860 metres
Days of racing – Mondays, Thursdays

SOUTH EAST

Aldershot
Oxenden Road
Tongham
Nr. Farnham
Tel: 0252 20182
Inside hare. Distances – 254, 462, 626, 842 metres
Days of racing – Wednesdays, Fridays

Bury St Edmunds
West Suffolk Stadium
Spring Lane
Bury St Edmunds
Suffolk
Tel: 0284 5163
Inside hare. Distances – 277, 471, 655, 877 metres
Days of racing – Thursdays, Saturdays

Clacton
Old Road
Clacton
Essex
Tel: 095 389 450
Outside hare. Distances – 213, 240, 404, 570, 600, 760, 925 metres
Days of racing – Tuesdays, Fridays

Huntingdon
Sapley Road
Hartford
Huntingdon
Tel: 0480 411474
Inside hare. Distances – 232, 393, 525, 716, 848 metres
Days of racing – Tuesdays, Fridays

Wisbech
South Brink
Wisbech
Cambs
Tel: 0945 585736
Inside hare. Distances – 286, 484, 700 metres
Days of racing – Wednesdays, Fridays

Appendix C – Useful Addresses, Treatments and Therapies

National Greyhound Racing Club Ltd,
24–28 Oval Road
London NW1 7DA
Tel: 01 267 9256/9

Veterinary Surgeons
Mrs Jeanne Jones MRCVS
Dunton Veterinary Clinic
Dunton Hall
Kingsbury Road
Curdworth
Sutton Coldfield
Warks
Tel: 0675 70322

David Poulter B.Vet. Med. MRCVS
64 Elmroyd Avenue
Potters Bar
Hertfordshire
Tel: 0707 54635

Bruce Prole MRCVS
309 Ongar Road
Brentwood
Essex
Tel: 0277 227462

Mr P. Sweeney
Wheatfield
Church Lawford
Nr. Rugby
Warks
Tel: 0203 542181

Osteopath
Mr R. Bradburn NDDO
Yew Tree Farm
Plant Lane
Moston
Sandbach
Tel: Warmingham 323

Grooming Aids
Flextol Ltd
Flextol Works
Ealing Green
London W5 5EL
Tel: 01 567 6444

Flextol can now offer their new CB45 grooming system which is larger than the original dog groomer, but using the fine black bristle brush similar results can be achieved as with their original groomer.

Stockists of foods and accessories for Greyhounds
Greyhound and Whippet Shop
288 Chingford Road
London E17
Tel: 01 527 7278

Don Pare
62 Mill Street
Barwell
Leicestershire LE9 8DW
Tel: 0455 43485

Rubbing Oils
CURACHO EMBROCATION

Sapo Acetate	4%
Phenol Camp	1.8%
Ol. Camph. Rect.	5%
Ol. Rosmarini	1%
Oil Sassafras	1.5%
Alcosolve add	100%

Curacho Company
Unit 4
Westover Trading Estate
Langport
Somerset

ALCO ECTOLIN EMBROCATION
Pexo Greyhound Veterinary Products Ltd
11a High Street
Welwyn
Herts AL6 9EE
Also available: Pexitone Tonic, Yellow Padsanol and White Padsanol.

RADIOL (M–R) LINIMENT
Radiol Chemicals Ltd
Stepfield
Witham
Essex CH8 3HG

To make Radiol spirit lotion
mix 60 ml each of Radiol (M–R) liniment and water with 300 ml methylated spirit. Contains Menthol BP 1.6% w/v; Camphor BP 0.6% w/v.

Duphapind (The answer to a fading puppy disease)
Duphar Ireland Ltd
Ballymount Drive
Walkinstown
Dublin 12
Tel: 01 521466

A new product recently launched for the prevention of puppy fading syndrome is Duphapind. Puppy fading syndrome is an apt term used to describe the way in which a litter of apparently healthy pups at birth literally fades away and dies usually within the first week. Greyhound breeders, and indeed breeders of most pet dogs, are familiar with the disease.

Duphapind is the result of many years of research by Duphar B.V. in Holland, in collaboration with Prof. A. Mayr at the Institute of Munich, West Germany. This research work was successful in producing an inactivated vaccine Duphapind. Duphapind has been shown to be a very effective paramunity inducer. There are many systems involved in paramunity but the principal one is the stimulation of interferon production (interferon inhibits virus replication).

Investigations into puppy deaths occurring soon after birth were also carried out by the UK Animal Health Trust in Newmarket and their work suggests that failure to produce or synthesise lung surfactant – the substance which allows normal respiratory adaptation to take place at birth – may be involved in fading puppy syndrome. Using Duphapind in their trials they found that the incidence of death due to fading puppy syndrome was dramatically reduced. Duphapind was given to bitches a week prior to whelping and also to the puppies as soon as possible after birth and then 24–48 hours later.

Any breeder that considers he may have a puppy fading problem in his kennels should consult his veterinary surgeon as Duphapind is now readily available.

Therapy Advisory Service
Blythe House
Blythe Lane
Lathom
Nr. Ormskirk
Lancashire L40 5UA
Tel: 0695 75139/79429

For a Greyhound to stay in peak condition, full spinal mobility is essential. If muscles are not fully and evenly exercised they will be unable to hold the skeletal structure in correct alignment. Massage with the Rollax a Mite is the answer. Simple to use, effective, safe and reliable, it gives all the benefits of regular, deep massage therapy, which is so strongly endorsed by leading vets and trainers.

Rollax a Mite is not a vibrator or an ultrasound apparatus. Its value lies in its massage effect. It is a light, uncomplicated and easy to use massager, so light in fact that even a child, given simple instructions, could use it effectively. The massaging heads of this equipment are adjustable, and they give a regular, deeply penetrating massage. Due to its intense massaging effect, the Rollax a Mite should not be applied to a group of muscles for longer than three minutes at any one session.

Sessions should be conducted twice daily for optimum results, i.e. morning and evening. One 3-minute session with a Rollax a Mite is equivalent to 25–30 minutes of hand massaging or rubbing, and any hard-working trainer or handler can see the benefits and time-saving advantage of such a system.

It is particularly effective in spinal massage and muscle conditioning. All in all it is a relatively inexpensive, easy to use, deep massager of great potential, and certainly a bonus in the hands of any serious owner or trainer.

Faradism and Ultrasound Treatment
FARADISM
Faradic stimulation has proved very successful for both developing and toning the muscles of the racing

Greyhound. A thorough daily muscle toning can easily and effectively be given for improved track performance in competition and, by the same process, considerably reduce exercising time. Individual muscles and tendons can be quickly checked and the local area of injury or soreness determined. Also as a pre-performance check, faradism has been found invaluable. After certain injuries muscle deterioration can be very quickly localised (e.g. to one leg, a shoulder or hip joint). Faradism can then be used to selectively develop the affected muscles thereby restoring correct balance.

Faradism (continuous or surged) is available on Stimsonic units where it can be applied independently or combined with ultrasound treatments.

The Mini-Faradic is a lightweight stimulator which can be used on its own or connected into the Vet-Sonic ultrasonic unit to provide similar combined therapy application as available on the Stimsonic.

ULTRASOUND

Ultrasound micro-massage is used effectively to increase the bloodflow to poorly supplied areas, e.g. tendons and ligaments. This can aid recovery after injury or help prevent injury prior to competition. Ultrasonic treatment is also extremely effective in improving lymph drainage, reducing soft swellings, draining open wound areas and reducing swollen joints.

Ultrasound not only increases the blood supply to affected areas, but also draws this towards the surface, aiding the speed of recovery of open wounds and reducing the formation of scar tissue.

Treatment of inflamed joints, hardened swellings (fibrosis), tendon injuries and pulled muscles is also possible with varying degrees of success according to the severity of the injury, but definite improvements can be seen with most cases within the first few treatments.

The rate of callous formation during the setting of fractured bones may be accelerated by treatment with ultrasound resulting in a speedier recovery.

Ultrasound is available on the Stimsonic and Vet-Sonic machines and is very easy to apply to Greyhounds either by direct contact or under water.

The faradic stimulation can be used very effectively to locate tender, painful areas on the Greyhound, and then these areas can be treated by the use of ultrasound. During the later stages of treatment when the dog is showing improvement, combined therapy can be given exercising the muscles around the treatment area, enabling an earlier return to racing.

The Stimsonic MK1V unit has four output modes: (a) ultrasound; (b) faradic; (c) combined; and (d) dual.

The Vet-Sonic unit has ultrasound output only, with provision for connecting to a Mini-Faradic unit for combined output.

The Mini-Faradic unit has faradic output only.

Obtainable from: R. A. Dodds (Electro
  Medical) Ltd
  12 Richmond Place
  Brighton BN2 2NA
  Tel: 0273 686096/686470

Ultrasound effects

It is generally agreed that ultrasound energy applied to human or animal bodies has four effects:

  (1) Mechanical
  (2) Chemical or Biological
  (3) Thermal

(1) Mechanical effects

This is really micro-massage in depth. Massage as a physical medicine modality has been used for very many centuries – certainly since the days of Hippocrates and probably earlier. In general terms massage exerts a series of pressures on body tissue and then releases and relaxes them. As has already been seen, ultrasound waves also produce pressures and when these are applied to soft tissue, they compress and release the tissue as in massage but at very much faster speeds. Also, because of the speed, they are able to effect micro-massage on tissue which would not produce a response to hand massage. Additionally, because of the controllability of the energy, it is possible to apply ultrasonic massage to areas on which it would be too painful to use hand massage. Another effect of these very fast sound waves is the oscillation of particles within the energy field. This is generally believed to improve blood circulation and lymphatic drainage of the site treated as well as loosening or disintegrating granules associated with rheumatic conditions.

(2) Chemical or Biological Effects

There are a number of chemical effects created by ultrasound waves and it is not the purpose here to go into this in detail. It will therefore be sufficient to list the more measurable biological reactions so that readers who are interested in such physiological effects will be acquainted with the primary processes involved.

It has been noted, both experimentally and through measurements made on live bodies, that the following chemical effects can be attributed to ultrasound irradiation:

(1) Improved permeability of all membranes to sodium and potassium ions.
(2) Inhibition of inflammatory processes.
(3) Vaso dilation.
(4) Analgesia.
(5) A change in tissue pH.
(6) Liberation of homochronologically active materials – transport of ions
(7) Improved hyperaemia.

(3) Thermal effects

The thermal effect or heat effect of ultrasound waves is really a by-product but nonetheless a very important one. The heat is produced by the friction created by the waves passing through the tissue. The advantage of this form of thermal activity against others in common use is that it is target heat. Infra-red rays, short waves and micro-waves have a more general heating effect on the whole of an area whereas ultrasound may be directed at the lesion itself.

Magnetic Field Therapy

Notes on the System MFT as supplied by
R. A. Dodds (Electro Medical) Ltd
12 Richmond Place
Brighton BN2 2NA
Tel: 0273 686096/686470

This is a much smaller unit than some of the early ones. It has four applicators so that two dogs can be treated at one time and the fasteners for the coat and the applicators are velcro tape. This is far easier than straps and buckles.

The cables are housed in special reels which minimise the chance of accidental damage and reduce the amount of cable lying on the floor. The liquid crystal display on the front panel of the generator provides instructions for the operator, and also indicates if and when there is a fault, either due to damage in the cable or incorrect connections. Full training can be given by arrangement. The price at present for the full Greyhound System is £1,050.00 plus Vat.

Appendix D – Bloodlines

```
                                              ┌─ Chief Havoc
                              ┌─ Rocket Fire ─┤
                              │                └─ Rose Fire
              ┌─ Rocket Ship ─┤
              │               │                ┌─ Oaklahoma
              │               └─ Lady Chee ───┤
              │                                └─ Ovetta
Bright Lad ──┤
              │                                ┌─ The Grand
              │                                │  Champion
              │               ┌─ Fourth of July┤
              │               │                └─ Little Toast
              └─ July Joan ───┤
                              │                ┌─ Explosive Gilbert
                              └─ Barbara Joan ─┤
                                               └─ Merely Mad
```

Bright Lad.

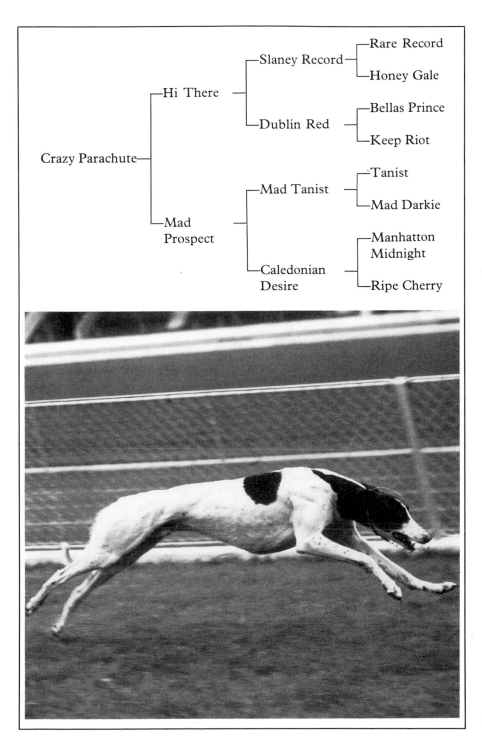

```
                                              ┌─Rare Record
                            ┌─Slaney Record──┤
                            │                 └─Honey Gale
              ┌─Hi There───┤
              │             │                 ┌─Bellas Prince
              │             └─Dublin Red──────┤
              │                               └─Keep Riot
Crazy Parachute─┤
              │                               ┌─Tanist
              │             ┌─Mad Tanist──────┤
              │             │                 └─Mad Darkie
              └─Mad         ┤
                Prospect    │                 ┌─Manhatton
                            │                 │  Midnight
                            └─Caledonian──────┤
                              Desire          └─Ripe Cherry
```

Crazy Parachut

Cricket Dance
- Prairie Flash
  - Hi There
    - Slaney Record
    - Dublin Red
  - Prairie Peg
    - The Grand Champion
    - Prairie Vixen
- Juggie
  - Man of Pleasure
    - Drumnam Rambler
    - Beauty of Pleasure
  - Midsummer Eve
    - Fourth of July
    - Look Pretty

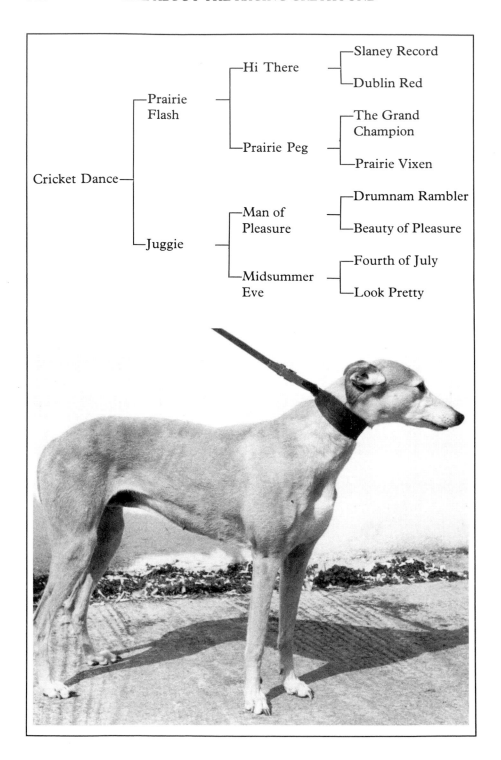

Cricket Dance.

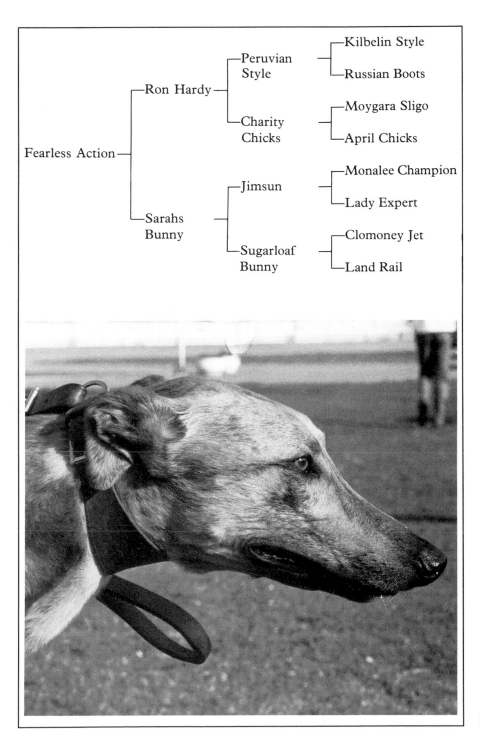

Fearless Action.

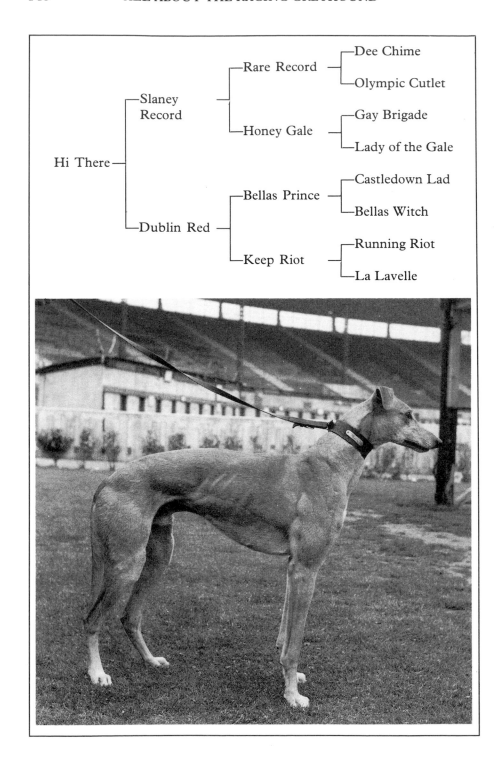

Hi There.

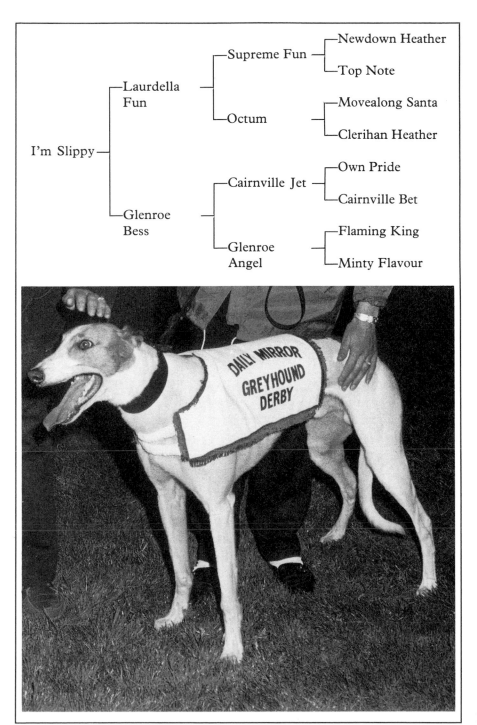

I'm Slippy.

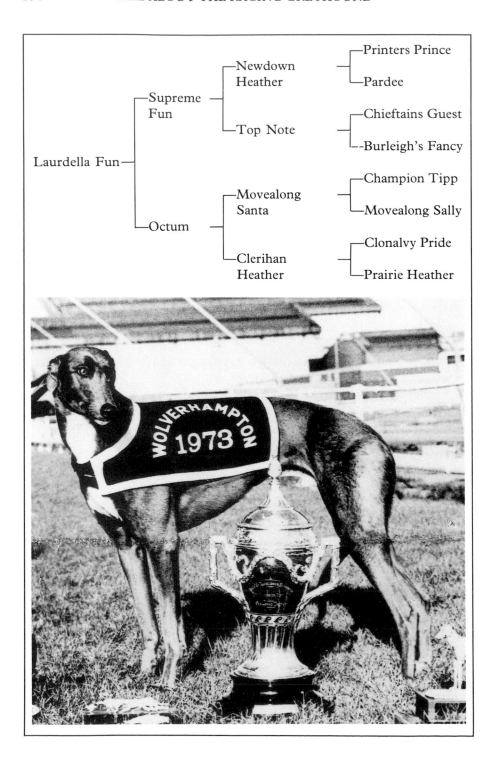

Laurdella Fun.

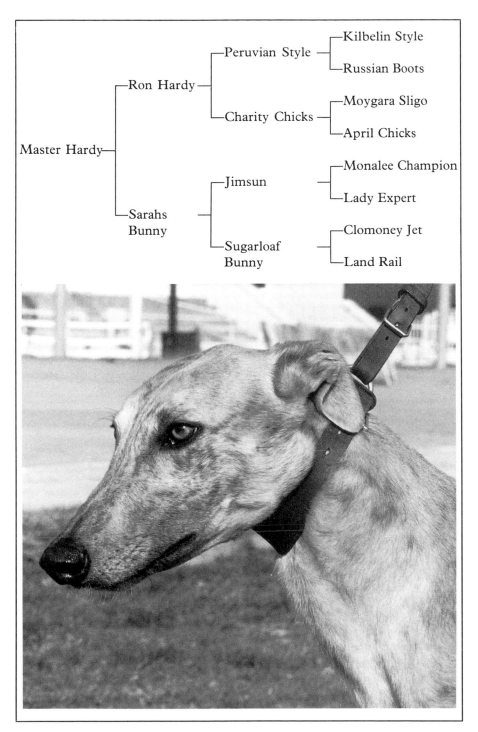

Master Hardy.

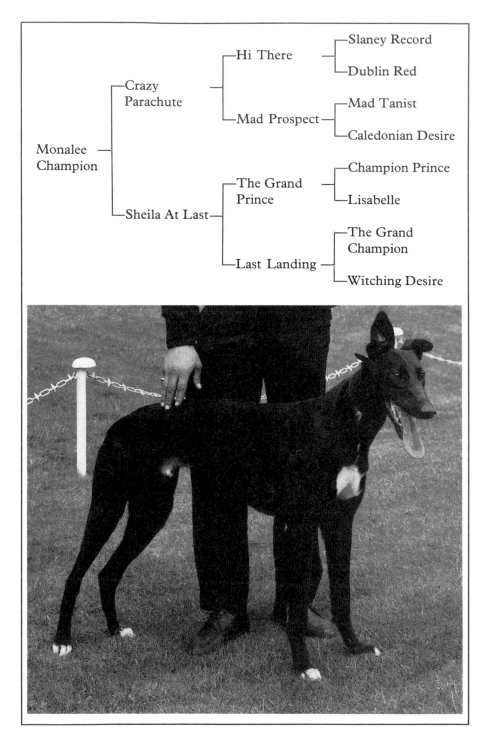

```
                                    ┌─Slaney Record
                        ┌─Hi There ─┤
              ┌─Crazy    │           └─Dublin Red
              │ Parachute┤
              │          │              ┌─Mad Tanist
              │          └─Mad Prospect─┤
Monalee ──────┤                         └─Caledonian Desire
Champion      │
              │                       ┌─Champion Prince
              │          ┌─The Grand ─┤
              │          │ Prince      └─Lisabelle
              └─Sheila At Last─┤
                         │              ┌─The Grand
                         └─Last Landing─┤  Champion
                                        └─Witching Desire
```

Monalee Champion.

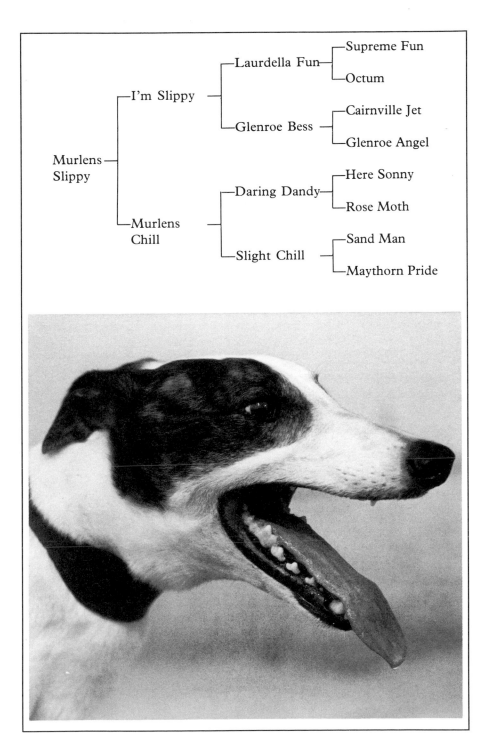

Murlens Slippy.

Myrtown.

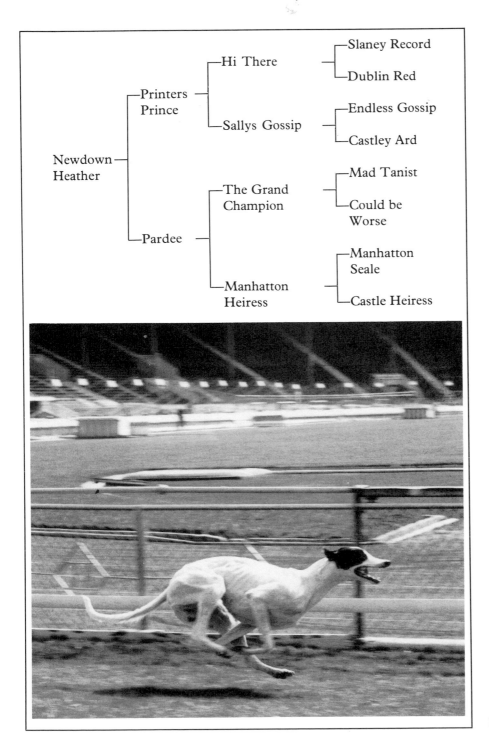

```
                              ┌─Slaney Record
                    ┌─Hi There─┤
          ┌─Printers ┤          └─Dublin Red
          │  Prince  │          ┌─Endless Gossip
          │          └─Sallys Gossip─┤
Newdown───┤                          └─Castley Ard
Heather   │                          ┌─Mad Tanist
          │          ┌─The Grand──────┤
          │          │  Champion      └─Could be
          └─Pardee───┤                   Worse
                     │                ┌─Manhatton
                     └─Manhatton──────┤  Seale
                        Heiress       └─Castle Heiress
```

Newdown Heather.

```
                                             ┌─Castledown
                              ┌─Bellas Prince─┤   Lad
                              │               └─Bellas Witch
             ┌─Champion───────┤
             │   Prince       │               ┌─Swanky Jog
             │                └─Sallywell──────┤
Pigalle Wonder─┤                              └─Lucy Lilla
             │                                 ┌─Mad Tanist
             │                ┌─The Grand──────┤
             │                │   Champion     └─Could be
             └─Prairie Peg────┤                    Worse
                              │                 ┌─Astras Son
                              └─Prairie Vixen───┤
                                                └─Take Murex
```

Pigalle Wonder.

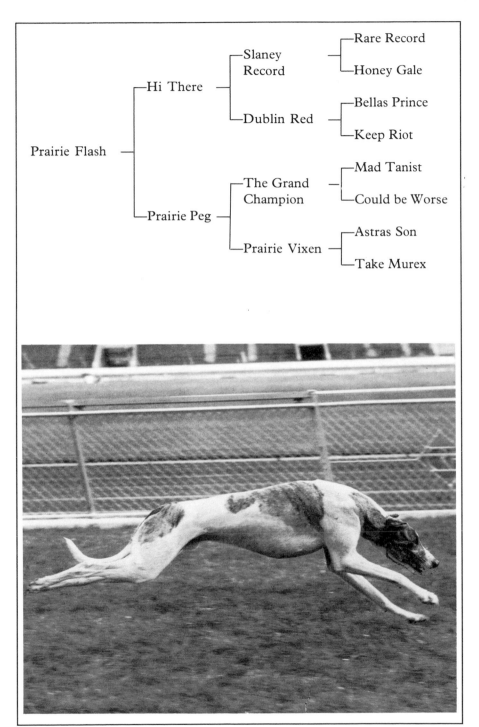

Prairie Flash.

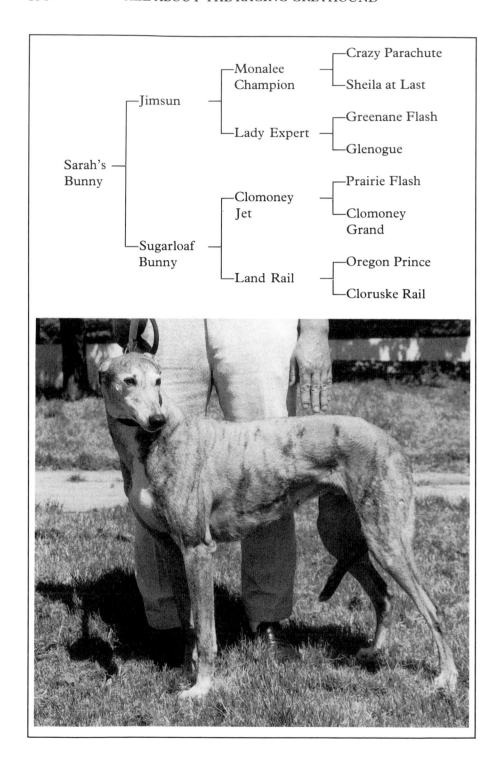

Sarah's Bunny.

```
                                          ┌─Ample Tip
                        ┌─My Friend        │
                        │  Lou             └─Win Dixie
           ┌─Friend     │
           │  Westy     │                  ┌─New World
           │            └─Westy            │
           │               Blubber         └─Kinto Nebo
Sandman ───┤
           │                               ┌─Rocket Jet
           │            ┌─Tell You Why     │
           │            │                  └─Gorgeous Babe
           └─Miss       │
              Gorgeous  │                  ┌─Mar Dilly
                        └─Miss Dilly       │
                           Mar             └─She's A Record
```

Sandman.

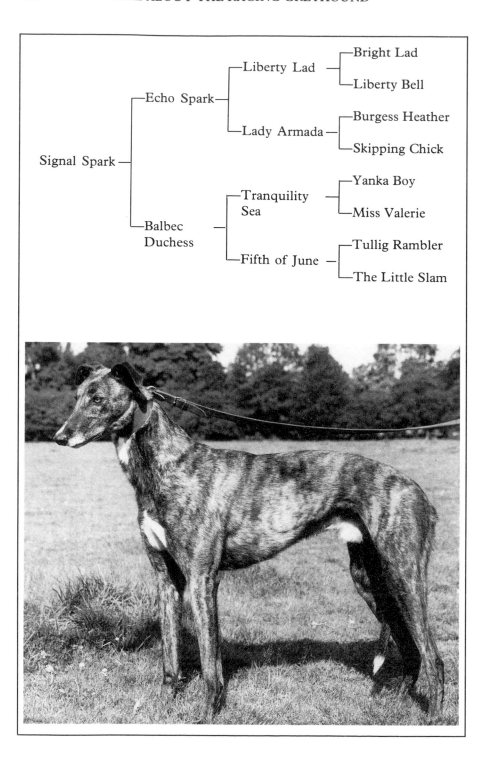

Signal Spark.

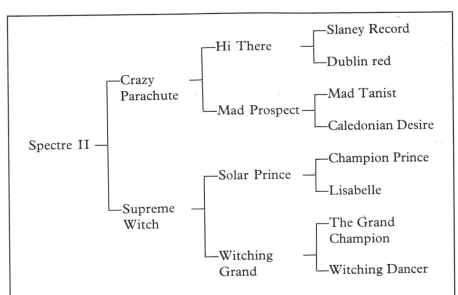

Also in this litter were Tric Trac, Forward King, Forward Flash

Spectre II.

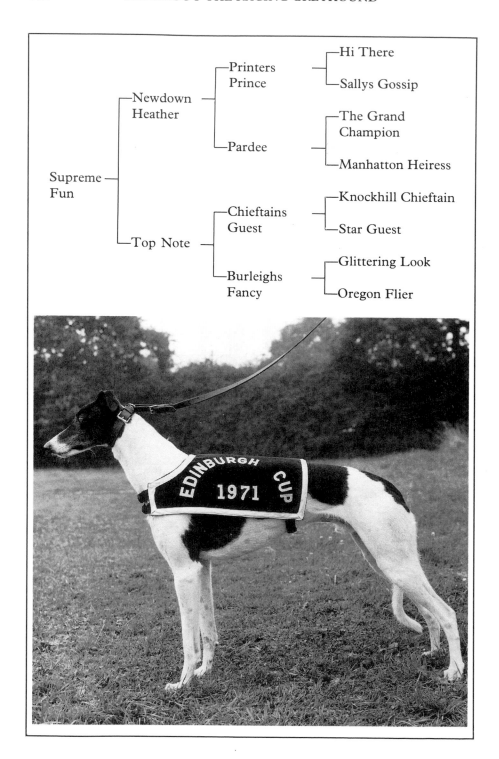

```
                                              ┌─Hi There
                             ┌─Printers       │
                             │ Prince ────────┤
              ┌─Newdown      │                └─Sallys Gossip
              │ Heather ─────┤
              │              │                ┌─The Grand
              │              │                │ Champion
              │              └─Pardee ────────┤
Supreme ──────┤                               └─Manhatton Heiress
Fun           │
              │                               ┌─Knockhill Chieftain
              │              ┌─Chieftains     │
              │              │ Guest ─────────┤
              └─Top Note ────┤                └─Star Guest
                             │
                             │                ┌─Glittering Look
                             └─Burleighs      │
                               Fancy ─────────┤
                                              └─Oregon Flier
```

Supreme Fun.

```
                                    ┌─Yanka Boy
                     ┌─Dark        ┤
                     │ Mercury     └─An Tain
          ┌─The     ┤
          │ Stranger │              ┌─Myross Again
          │          └─Lovely Blend ┤
          │                         └─Clomoney Star
Tico ─────┤
          │                         ┌─Monalee Champion
          │          ┌─Linda's     ┤
          │          │ Champion     └─Merry Linda
          └─Derry   ┤
            Linda    │              ┌─Kilbelin Style
                     └─Ballinderry ┤
                       Moth         └─Skipping Chick
```

Tico.

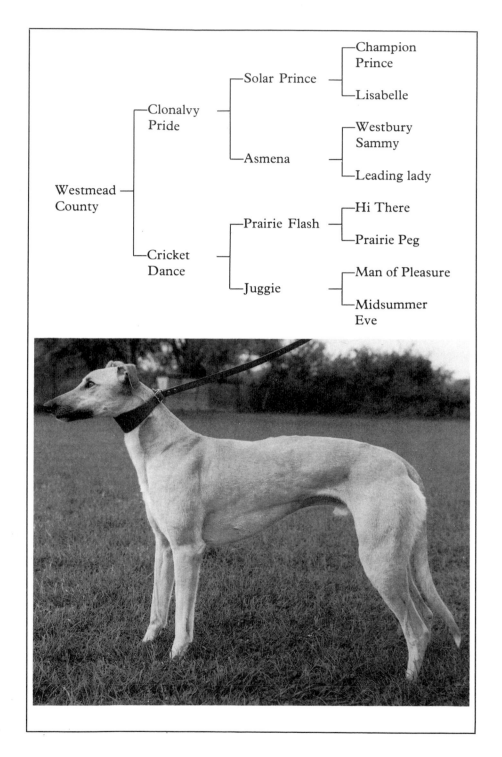

Westmead County.

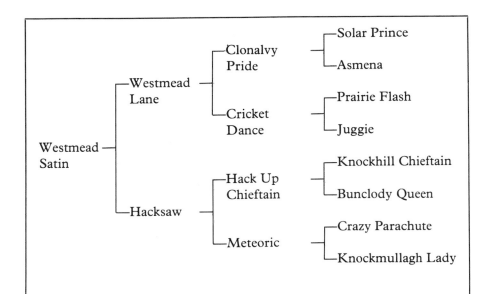

```
                                                        ┌─Solar Prince
                                        ┌─Clonalvy
                                        │  Pride     └─Asmena
                        ┌─Westmead ─────┤
                        │  Lane         │            ┌─Prairie Flash
                        │               └─Cricket
                        │                  Dance     └─Juggie
      Westmead ─────────┤
      Satin             │                            ┌─Knockhill Chieftain
                        │               ┌─Hack Up
                        │               │  Chieftain └─Bunclody Queen
                        └─Hacksaw ──────┤
                                        │            ┌─Crazy Parachute
                                        └─Meteoric
                                                     └─Knockmullagh Lady
```

Westmead Satin.

Index

Numbers in bold type refer to illustrations.